A RUSSIAN JOURNEY

Moscow: inside the Kremlin

A RUSSIAN JOURNEY

From Suzdal to Samarkand

Text by Alaric Jacob
Drawings by Paul Hogarth

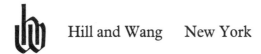 Hill and Wang   New York

Published in the United States of America by
Hill and Wang, Inc.

STANDARD BOOK NUMBER: 8090–8350–7

LIBRARY OF CONGRESS CATALOG CARD NUMBER: 68–30795

FIRST AMERICAN EDITION JUNE 1969

Designed and produced by
Charles Rosner & Associates Limited London

Printed in England by
Lund Humphries, London and Bradford

CONTENTS

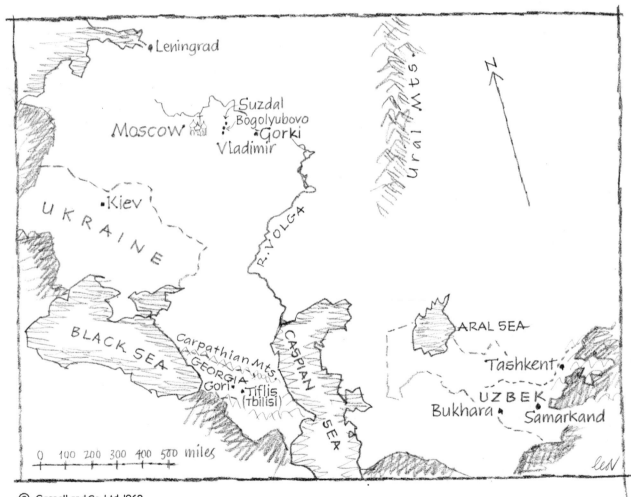

Leningrad

Suzdal
Bogolyubovo
Moscow
Gorki
Vladimir

Kiev

U K R A I N E

R. VOLGA

Ural Mts.

N

BLACK SEA

Carpathian Mts.

GEORGIA

Gori
Tiflis
(Tbilisi)

CASPIAN SEA

ARAL SEA

Tashkent

U Z B E K
Bukhara
Samarkand

0 100 200 300 400 500 miles

1 THE REASONS WHY

It is a truth universally acknowledged that any man who writes a book about the Soviet Union should start with an apology for adding yet another mite to an already over-ripe cheese. Having already written extensively about the Soviet Union there would have been no excuse for writing more had I made this journey alone. But what follows is a joint production – the first for very many years by artist and writer working in Russia together. I first went to Russia in 1943 soon after the battle of Stalingrad, fortified by two years in the Western Desert culminating in the victory of Alamein, and I remained there, on and off, until the Cold War began in the winter of 1947. At this point I returned to England and had no direct contact with Russia for twenty years, though I served for a while as a pressed man in a sort of land-based cold warship whose inmates called it H.M.S. Kremlinologist. When my so-called expertise withered away, as it soon did, I was glad to return to more honest forms of journalism. Yet, just as he who has once drunk the waters of the Nile will always return, so I looked forward to going back to Russia one day. I never imagined it would take so long.

The origin of this book can be traced back to a day nearly twenty years ago when Paul Hogarth moved into the unused top floor of my house at Hampton Court. At that time I had just published a book about Russia in wartime and my first wife, Iris Morley, had enjoyed the greatest success of her short life as a writer* with *Soviet Ballet*, which made the Western world

* She died in 1953

aware for the first time that the startling impact made by Diaghilev before the first World War represented only a part of the balletic riches of Russia and that the great traditions of the Maryinsky and the Bolshoi had not succumbed to the cutting-off of Imperial patronage but had in fact been strengthened by the Soviet régime. Paul and I decided that one day we would travel through Russia together with sketch-book and typewriter, with no set programme, and in a picaresque spirit make use of whatever came our way.

We knew just how it should be. Yet it was not to be. The Cold War made it impossible for anyone from the West to wander freely around Russia in the way we had planned. Nor was it only the Russians who were suspicious. After the Fulton speech it became quite fashionable in England to accept Churchill's belief that the second World War had been unnecessary, the war that need never have happened had the appeasers been exposed in time and the semi-Fascist Polish Government of Colonel Beck prevented from blocking a genuine alliance between Russia and the West. But to believe that the Cold War was even more unnecessary because it was inconceivable that Russia with her ruined economy and her twenty million dead could possibly contemplate an attack on the West – this was unpardonable heresy. All who proclaimed this belief became marked men. Publishers did not want our books, newspapers had no use for our articles, the radio was closed to us. So it went on for many years. Yet we had confidence that one day the climate would change. In 1958, Paul took part in an exhibition of British art at the Pushkin Gallery in Moscow and went there with two of his fellow exhibitors, George Fullard and Derrick Grieves. But they were so lavishly entertained that they could do no work and it was still not possible for either of us to travel freely.

We might, of course, have carried out our project in another country. Paul began to fulfil many commissions in the United States: I had worked in Washington before the war, I had a Bostonian grandmother and relations in several states of the Union – we could have had all the introductions we needed and far better facilities than would ever have been available in Russia. But although in childhood games I had chosen the United States as my second country while my brother chose Japan (their picturesque emblems among the Flags of all Nations at the back of the atlas governed our choice) I had no desire to go to America now. Russia it had to be. I had been mixed up with Russia for most of my life, for two interlocking reasons. The first reason, for many people growing up between the wars, was that Russia represented the spirit of the times. The generation of Rupert Brooke and Raymond Asquith had posed the question: 'How does one lead life to the full?' But between the wars, when the Bright Young People, wearing baby clothes, were being pushed in perambulators to one another's parties while the teeth of the workless rotted in their mouths and Ramsay MacDonald soared 'on and on and on and up and up and up' and unemployment rose to three millions, the *Zeitgeist* posed a different question. 'How does one change the world?' we asked. And the search for an answer drew many of us towards the East. The study of Marx became obligatory. Everyone was doing it, from Harold Macmillan to the Dean of Canterbury. Even Lady Astor and Mary Pickford found it essential to visit Russia, carried there by the pregnant phrase of Lincoln Steffens, so often derided and yet ever-challenging: 'I have seen the future, and it works.'

To some, of course, Marxism became the new religion – the opium of the intellectuals – and Russia the Holy Land to which disillusioned relicts of Christianity directed their steps. Even in 1947 a Left-wing Labour M.P. told me, when I urged him to visit Russia instead of only reading about it: 'I don't think I have the courage. It would be terrible if I were to lose my faith.'

This general trend was reinforced, for me, by a private imperative. I grew up in a circle which for generations had 'served overseas' rather than worked at home. My family and their friends constituted a sort of imperial guard. Landless gentry, for the most part, for whom England had become too small generations before it had shrunk to its present claustrophobic proportions, they found it necessary to acquire a second country where they could spend most of their lives remote from the restrictions of Subtopia. They had, indeed, very little use for England except as a place to die in. As Political Resident at Aden, my father had as second country the Yemen and when, in the first World War, he served in Allenby's Arab Bureau in Cairo he and his friends each enjoyed the luxury of having a country, even a potentate, of their own. St. John Philby had Ibn Saud, T. E. Lawrence had Faisal, and my father had the King of the Yemen, Imam Yahya. Greatly envying this state of affairs, but being too young to aspire towards it, my brother and I invented second countries of our own, for which we drew maps, produced newspapers and a *Who's Who*, wrote the Prime Minister's speeches, laid out railways, and, of course, conducted sanguinary wars. In my teens I called my country Neurasthenia but this was *esprit d'escalier*; at its foundation it bore the unoriginal name of Estonia, after the homeland of our cook-housekeeper, a splendid woman named Mrs. Birse whose kindly rule exposed us to the gastronomic delights of *bliny* and *Kotleti po Kievski* at a time when our contemporaries were sitting down to a cut from the joint and two veg. The image of Russia derived from Mrs. Birse was of a dramatic country

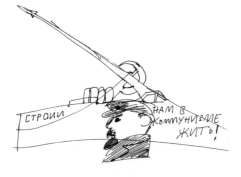

whose people lived fuller lives, knew keener joys and sorrows than did the English gentry in their parallel course of imperial decline. When I first went to Russia many years later I found that Mrs. Birse's projection was essentially true. And as I flew up to Moscow from Teheran in 1943, who should be sitting next to me but Mrs. Birse's stepson, Arthur, a British major who was to become Churchill's interpreter in all his meetings with Stalin.

And, to complete the pattern of involvement, who should I find installed at Moscow on my present visit but the son of my father's old friend of Arabian days who had spent holidays with us in the Weald of Kent and enjoyed Mrs. Birse's *bliny* as much as we did – the late pride of *The Times*, the Foreign Office and the British Secret Service, Kim Philby. Though, to be sure, Kim had carried his search for a second country somewhat farther than I had done.

Moscow: the Yaroslavsky railway station

2 TWENTY YEARS AFTER

We chose a Tupolev jet of Aeroflot rather than the B.E.A. Comet, and found it to be a bigger and more comfortable aircraft although its appointments were less elegant and its service was to prove much inferior. And yet, though the cabin smelt of dust and disinfectant, we had never travelled so spaciously before. We had heard that the Managing Director of the multiple tailors Montagu Burton and his export team might be on our flight with a view to signing an export order for half-a-million pounds' worth of British suits, but in fact an old Russian lady bringing her grandchild home from Washington was our only fellow passenger and when she disappeared into the first class Paul and I had the rest of the aircraft to ourselves. The décor was grey with green rep seats. As we took off an empty wine bottle hurtled rearwards from the galley amidships and careered down the aisle towards the tail. Paul and I burst out laughing together, both exclaiming: 'Typical!' I was reminded of some of the mad flights I had taken in Soviet Dakotas during the war when, the army seating being insufficient, overstuffed armchairs had been introduced into the cabin, with the result that when the plane climbed steeply after take-off, the chairs were thrown towards the tail and their occupants were fortunate not to break a leg. We banked steeply over Windsor Castle and Eton and were reminded that the Royal family must be among the principal sufferers from jet noise in the country. But the privations of the Queen and her consort did not long oppress our spirits. It was a lovely cold day of early Spring with crisp sunshine which promised to make England and Denmark co-exist in the clear ambiance of

Scandinavia. The three air hostesses took no interest in us to begin with. Lunch came in its own good time – Russian time, that is, about two o'clock in the afternoon – as we were well out over the North Sea. The menu provided a little caviar, cold ham and a mayonnaise salad, roast chicken, Danish potato balls and the inevitable frozen peas, Australian butter and some very British processed cheese and an even more British pastry for which we could not blame the Russians but rather the catering people at London Airport. We had some excellent red wine from Georgia free of charge and some good strong coffee. The tablecloth and napkins were of fine linen. The standard aimed at seemed to be one of solid comfort – with no luxury. No attempt was made to sell us French perfumes, cigarettes, or duty-free drink as is done on the Comet, which was odd because every *Intourist* Hotel in Russia has its shop where luxuries are sold for foreign currencies and this system could easily be extended to Soviet international flights.

We crossed the sandy shoreline of Jutland and the sky took on that marvellous Nordic transparency – bluer than a Mediterranean sky and more sparkling, because of the cold.

Spending a penny over the Baltic introduced us to the very Russian character of the Tupolev's loo. Much larger than that on a British aircraft, it was rather like a washroom on an American pullman car with a green-upholstered sofa running along one wall. Only the brass cuspidor on the floor was lacking. The privy lay behind a door with top and bottom missing as in a Wild West saloon. No lunatic could have locked himself in there, armed or with suicidal intent, without being spotted and, if need be, rescued over the top.

The weather continued to sparkle as we passed over the Gulf of Riga but as we began to intrude upon the great Russian land mass the earth became brown with evergreen forests stretching haphazardly to the horizon. Where the forests ended the land was stippled over with belts of snow like white paint capriciously sprayed over a brown abstract with the mirror-glass of frozen lakes in between. Even over these populous Baltic republics one had an impression of immense space. We criticize Russia as a regimented country yet every Russian enjoys a vast territory in which to evade his quota of regimentation. Living in Russia may, and I think does produce a number of disagreeable sensations among those of sensitive temperament but claustrophobia is not one of them. However constricted his own backyard may be, every Russian is conscious of an immense hinterland beyond it whereas we in England are as tightly packed as toys in a rich child's nursery. When I attend an international conference these days I feel that the U.K. delegation should be renamed the U.C. delegation. Since we shed our empire we have dwindled into a United Conurbation and, to anyone who loves travel as much as I do, this is profoundly sad.

Coming in to land at Sheremeteyvo airport, a wintry sun hung low over a counterpane of cloud, but after we had dived through it we found ourselves in a nether world: snow was falling from a pewter sky and the forest surrounding the frozen runway looked purple in the fading light. After our sunlit flight it was a depressing *coup de théâtre*: one felt as if one had just been shattered by bad news. We taxied towards a cylindrical control tower of Scandinavian aspect. The door was opened by a frontier guard in his green cap and an Aeroflot girl led our tiny party over some quarter-mile of snowy tarmac to the main building – a vast empty temple clean and brightly lit, dedicated to some future means of international air travel still many years ahead. There were not more than eight travellers all told in this huge place and the formalities could not have been simpler.

A car awaited us and we were on our way into Moscow within ten minutes. The narrow road from the airport passed through wooded country before joining a great motorway. In the fields on either side we saw wooden cottages nearly all bearing television aerials even though most of them seemed not to have been painted for years and some had crazy roofs and eaves on the verge of collapse. Harsh electric light burst out of each house and lit up the surrounding snow. In a landscape untidy and forbidding each cottage stood out as an outpost of human warmth and jollity in the wintry waste. I was forcibly reminded of the madness of Hitler and his generals in trying to overrun and occupy thousands of square miles of such country in the depth of winter. At that time no lights ever shone over the snow: ruin and desolation lay all around. Presently we passed a memorial, composed of anti-tank barriers painted the colour of blood, which marks the spot where Guderian's tanks were halted on the outskirts of Moscow in the winter of 1941.

I had no idea from which quarter we were approaching the city and even had I known I would never have recognized the area, so great were the changes twenty years had brought about. When I looked at the map later I realized that the district of huge apartment blocks and wide avenues we were now entering had in my day been the quiet village of Khimki where we used to go swimming in the summer months. I was instantly reminded of the Bronx. These buildings were cruder – they had been built in a tearing hurry during the fourteen years since Stalin died and one could detect at a glance the buildings of more grandiose style left over from the Stalin era – and yet these avenues were very reminiscent of New York, with their huge shop fronts running the full length of the street frontage. We drove down the broad avenue at fifty miles an hour, mile after mile. A whole new city stood on what had in my time been allotments and market gardens. And this had happened along each of the seven or eight avenues which finally converge like the spokes of a wheel at the Kremlin in the heart of the city. A circular motorway sixty miles long now marks the limits of the metropolis. Outside this a belt of forest and parkland has been preserved: within, all the old wooden houses are being torn down; no individual homes whatever are being built – only great apartment blocks and offices. No city in the world is being reconstructed upon such a scale. Of Moscow's more than six million people no fewer than six hundred thousand are building workers and the rebuilding is far from finished yet. I could feel no aesthetic pleasure over construction on such a scale, which seemed likely to destroy the ancient character of Moscow by making its citizens lead the same sort of sub-metropolitan existence as in the poorer parts of any American city. I thought of the cynical young man in the American Embassy who had said to me in 1943: 'You know why we're fighting this war? So that, in the long run, the people of Moscow will be able to live just like the Polacks and Wops in Detroit.' And I wondered if he would crow over the scene before me now. And yet, when I remembered how families in Moscow once had to be satisfied with a couple of rooms, and often only one, all this must be set down as progress.

At the National Hotel – where Lenin had lived when he first came to Moscow in 1918 after moving the government from St. Petersburg – I saw with misgiving that an annexe being built at the back stretched some way up Gorki Street. I wondered if the big, old-fashioned rooms in the front with their wonderful views over the Kremlin and full of the charm of that period when Tsarist Russia and Edwardian England went through a common allegiance to *art nouveau* were being retained for de luxe class visitors at twelve pounds a day while tourists like ourselves were pushed into the annexe. And so it proved to be. We were to spend an indignant night in cell-like rooms at the back until the management, yielding to our shameless plea that we were on a 'cultural mission', moved us into modest singles at the front where we had a real bath next day instead of a shower and where my cupboard boasted a coat hanger inscribed *Claridges – London*.

Roaming round the hotel, which Paul remembered as the Algonquin of Moscow, we found a bar where foreign currency only was tender. Here we bought two vodkas and a plate of *sakuski* for fifteen shillings. The furnishing of the place suggested the annexe of a bingo parlour in Blackpool. A huge refrigerator proudly labelled MOCKBA occupied the place of honour between two pretty plump barmaids and a juke-box made in Poland was playing what sounded like watered-down Beatle music from the people's democracies. As our travels progressed we were to find these juke boxes in so many inappropriate places that Paul called them 'Poland's revenge'. The hotel dining-room, too, was a betrayal of its old self. No trace of the Algonquin here. It looked as if it were about to be demolished, which it probably is, for a far larger room will be needed when the annexe is completed. The lighting was like that in a garage, the food – when it came – was lukewarm, tasteless and expensive. A dark woman in black lace sang light operatic numbers with the band. Few Russians were present and I knew that something must be wrong. For Russians, like the French, have a natural appreciation of food and will travel some distance to find a good restaurant rather than put up with a bad one.

Afterwards, as the snow began to set in for the evening, we walked around the centre of the city. Twenty years had not in any way lessened the splendour of Theatre Square with all its classical stages. The Bolshoi remains for me the grandest opera house in the world but I noticed a sad falling-off in the character of the nearby Metropole Hotel, where I had lived during and after the war. I walked into the lobby and could not recognize it because the Edwardian décor had been ripped out and travel posters on cardboard mountings substituted, as if for some transient exhibition. And I missed the undraped, life-sized female figure on the stairs who never quite lit my way to bed for the lamp of liberty she held aloft was usually extinct, some hooligan having stolen the bulb. I was saddened, too, to see the facade of the Grand Hotel in darkness. This had once been the most elegant hotel in Moscow: in 1947, as President of the Association of Anglo-American Correspondents, I had wound up that body at the onset of the Cold War with a farewell luncheon there that would have done credit to the Berkeley in London, which it somewhat resembled: now its ironwork was rusty and broken, its entrance shuttered. Its roof carried an illuminated sign advertising the merits of the Moskva Hotel round the corner, which is doubtless about to swallow it up.

In Red Square the floodlit Kremlin towers behind Lenin's tomb looked as splendid as ever.

'You must have seen some strange sights here during the war', said Paul.

I had, indeed. There was the Victory Parade when the captured standards of the German Army were carried into the square by Russian generals and cast down on the paving-stones at Stalin's feet . . . There was VE day itself when all traffic came to a halt for twenty-four hours because the whole centre of the city was choked by millions of people dancing in the streets . . . When I came off the Arctic convoy at Archangel they had given me a 'red duster' with the injunction 'Wave this

flag for the Merchant Navy in the Moscow Victory Parade'; on VE day I had managed to get into Red Square on a British Army station wagon waving my old red flag with the Union Jack quartered on it while a Red Army major sat on the bonnet singing 'Tipperary', fifteen Russian children were singing on the roof, Alexander Werth was standing on the running-board shouting 'Slava' to every institution and individual he could think of in all the Russias and Adam Watson of the British Embassy was weaving through the crowd waving a red flag in one hand and the Union Jack in the other. 'Get down off that car!' the crowd shouted when they saw my British uniform, intending to throw me up in the air in the old Slav style. But I had no desire to meet the fate of the old Dean of Canterbury, whom I had just seen being tossed in the air in a blanket, his gaitered legs flailing thin air – the very image of a clown on a trampoline.

Between the vast GOUM department store where twenty thousand people can shop at one time and Ivan the Terrible's splendid Cathedral of St. Basil Paul and I were approached by two young men. One looked well-bred and diffident and remained silent during the ensuing conversation. The other, a dark Southern type possessed of a few words of English, matched his stride with ours and embarked on a long monologue about the absolute necessity for him to 'emigrate from this dreadful country'. In the old days I would have set the pair down at once as *agent provocateur* and attendant witness, but this youth seemed too unbalanced by unhappiness to be worth employing in such a role.

'Is it possible to speak free with you?' he demanded. 'Can you perhaps help me leave for America, or for England?'

Paul and I were non-committal.

'I have no future here,' he went on. 'My father is a colonel in the Army – an ultra-Communist who believes every word of our government. But I cannot do that. To me our government is a nonsense. It utters absurdities unchanged since Stalin's day. I must tell you that I despise my father and his friends.'

'Sons despise their fathers in England, too,' I assured him.

'The old man welcomes my call-up to the Army but I want to escape before that happens.'

'If you could get to America,' I said, 'you might be called up there too. And then you'd find yourself fighting in Vietnam. Would you like that?'

'Only one year's fighting in Vietnam is better than three years' call-up here.'

'Don't you want to live?' asked Paul.

'Yes, but only in freedom.'

'I am an Englishman with a son,' I said, 'and I would rather he served in the Soviet Army in peacetime than went to fight for the Americans in Vietnam. Last time we all fought a just war together but now one of us fights a dirty war alone.'

'You advise me then to go to England which does not fight at present?'

I was growing tired of a conversation the idiocy of which was not due to the young man's linguistic shortcomings but to his utter lack of native wit.

'Surely you must see,' I said, 'that we can't possibly help you to emigrate. If you wish to go abroad you must find your own way to it.'

Hardly had we shaken off these satellites than another young man approached us and enquired if we wished to see some pictures.

'Dirty ones, no doubt,' said I to Paul.

'No,' said the young man in well-modulated English, 'sacred ones.'

Beyond St. Basil's lay the new Rossia Hotel, destined, when completed, to be the biggest in the world with accommodation for six thousand guests. The first section had recently been opened. Blazing with light, it looked well-built and tastefully designed and furnished. A garden was being laid out at the entrance and to one side an old church with golden domes was being restored. Later we heard that many Russian architects feared that the great length of the building along the embankment of the Moskva River would dwarf the Kremlin when viewed from the south bank of the river but the elevation had been kept low and our first impression was favourable. We went to the restaurant where a dinner dance was going on. Plenty of Soviet champagne was being drunk. The women were well dressed and the men's dark blue suits and nylon shirts were well above the standards of Montagu Burton. The bar, on the balcony level, was very small, with ten stools and only one barmaid. I knew it was *ne kulturny* to stand at a bar and in fact so long as we were standing by apologetically the barmaid made no attempt to serve us. Our difficulty was spotted by two of the drinkers – one turned out to be a journalist from Rostov-on-Don and the other an engineer from Kiev – and we were offered a half-share of their stools. These could not possibly have supported two pairs of buttocks but by propping up one half on each, all four of us became entitled to drink.

The man from Rostov said: 'Tonight the vodka is present – the wife far away: tomorrow the situation will be reversed and I shall have a hangover.' He then tried to tell us a dirty story about

Moscow: St. Basil's Cathedral

Nelson and Lady Hamilton but as the point depended upon a Russian pun he found the task beyond him. There was about these exchanges a complete absence of familiarity but rather a kind of respectful though humorous approach to two foreigners that was profoundly well-mannered. Such an attitude is very Russian. I have occasionally in Russia encountered a rude approach from a stranger but never once has this persisted – even in a drunken man – once it was established that I was what is invariably termed 'a foreign guest'.

Next morning I spent a couple of hours by the telephone trying to make as many contacts as possible. The results were not merely disappointing, they were alarming. Paul had gone out early in the hope of starting work in the Kremlin. He had at least seventy drawings to make and only one month in which to do them all. But it was snowing and he was soon driven back to the hotel. Even in the shelter of an archway it was too cold to hold a pencil. But he wasn't too disappointed. 'Let us see as many people as we can today, while the weather's bad. Who shall we see first?'

I had to tell him not one single person was available. The telephone service, which had been bad enough twenty years before, was now far worse because there were plainly not enough lines to carry a far greater volume of traffic. I was to find that many busy offices, with a telephone on every desk, had only one outside line to carry all the calls. Even the *Intourist* girls in the service bureau of the National Hotel, who were on the phone from morning till night, had to share one line between two. Paul and I had few letters of introduction. The Soviet Writers Union and the USSR–Great Britain Society had been told we were coming. That was all. But whether they would help us, and to what extent, it was impossible to discover because I could not get the right people on the phone. We were not 'sponsored' in any way; we had come as ordinary tourists, though spending far more than the average tourist because we were travelling independently. Paul and I looked at one another with expressions of mock alarm designed, I was sure, to conceal a genuine panic. Had we made an appalling mistake in coming here in this free-and-easy manner, relying in the main on contacts I had made twenty and more years before? I had been confident of being able to locate Olga and Valentina and Mikhail Vladimirovich and Sava Gregorevich and many more. But Mikhail was dead: his widow, whom I had never met, had just told me so. And the others had vanished as though they had never been, their telephone numbers had been taken over by strangers. Even the twin *doyens* of the foreign press corps, my old colleagues Henry Shapiro and Edmund Stevens, whose long service in Moscow surpassed that of the legendary Walter Duranty and Thomas Cholerton of pre-war days, were not available – Shapiro was in

India and Stevens in England. I had drawn a complete blank. If this negative response continued, there would be no book.

'We mustn't lose heart,' I said without much conviction. 'We're trying to do something that hasn't been done for generations. If it was easy it wouldn't be worth doing. Russia's always been a damned difficult country. Remember Remington!'

The American artist Frederic Remington was one of Paul's heroes. He it was who had the famous telegraphic exchange with William Randolph Hearst when sent to Cuba in 1898 to cover the Spanish–American war. To his cable: 'I can find no war', Hearst replied: 'You furnish the pictures: I'll furnish the war.' His visit to Russia in 1892 was a cautionary tale which offered consolation to us now. He and his friend, the journalist Poulteney Bigelow, the editor of *Outing*, arrived in St. Petersburg with a big commission from *Harper's Monthly*. They planned to journey down the Volga in two Rob Roy canoes equipped with sails and water-tight compartments to hold paper and artists' materials. They hoped to launch their canoes on the Neva but despite innumerable visits to the American Embassy and to the Home Office the customs would not release the vessels and meanwhile they were followed everywhere and their letters had obviously been opened and clumsily re-sealed. Remington concluded that 'the Russian Government was very jealous of foreigners who came to report on things Russian'. They were told they had come 'on a fool's errand' and after being denied the necessary travel permits they were 'politely requested to disappear from Russia in the shortest possible time'. When their canoes were eventually released the hulls were found to be riddled with holes. Deciding that they might legitimately sail down the Volga in the regular steamer on their way home, they found themselves still under surveillance. Remington made sketches of houses, trees and cattle from the moving steamer but when told by a security officer that this was not allowed, Remington tossed his notebooks into the Volga, declaring: 'I don't mind being shot, Big, but don't let them lock me up in a damp cell.'

And so Frederic Remington – who rode with the U.S. Cavalry to depict the struggle with the hostile Plains Indians – left Russia without a single drawing to compensate for all the weeks he had wasted.

Fortified in our resolve by this recollection, we set out to walk through the snow to the Pushkin Museum where Paul, on his last visit in 1958, had taken part in the official exhibition, 'Looking at People'. Today the Museum was crowded and we were at once reminded of one of the

climatic handicaps which every Russian institution has to face – the need to make elaborate provision for winter clothing. In the basement of the museum a cloakroom ran the full length of the building, staffed by half a dozen old women and large enough to stack hundreds of fur coats and winter boots at one time. The space given over to this function could have housed another gallery.

Upstairs the visitors included a high proportion of private soldiers and airmen on leave. There were a number of parents with children just old enough not to be a nuisance and one or two very pretty girls with their admirers who, from the amorous looks being exchanged, seemed to be telling them that they were more beautiful than any of the pictures.

In the gallery devoted to modern French painting there were three magnificent Picassos of the blue period and some splendid works by Matisse, Gauguin, Utrillo, Fernand Léger and the Douanier Rousseau. All the French artists who were members of the Communist Party have had shows in the Soviet Union since Stalin died – Picasso, Matisse, Léger and Marcel Gromaire, and in addition Picasso has given to the Pushkin some of his best pottery, but the genesis of the French collection – of which only the tip of the iceberg is shown at the Pushkin with more at the Hermitage in Leningrad – lies in the work of two Russian millionaires of the Edwardian era – Sergei Shchukin, the railway magnate, and Ivan Morosov, the sugar king. These two made frequent trips to Paris in the early years of the century and were so well advised as to buy these enormously valuable works at a time when they could be had cheap. What Gertrude Stein collected piecemeal through friendship and personal involvement in the movement these two Muscovite tycoons bought wholesale, with the result that the Soviet Union now possesses a collection of post-Impressionist and modern French paintings second to none in the world. When I asked the curator whether any attempt had been made to insure the collection she said they were worth so many millions of pounds sterling that it would be difficult even for Lloyd's to cover them. For years the paintings lay in crates in the Pushkin or were hung like disused scenery from 'flies' in the restoration room of the museum. How many masters of the modern school of Paris remain unseen in Russia is not disclosed. But soon the staid old Tretyakov Gallery is to build an extension to house modern art from all over Europe. Then we shall see.

Paul maintains that the origin of the trauma which led to the ostracism of modern art in Russia and the dominance for a whole generation of the socialist–realist school of Gerasimov and kindred academic hacks was not ideological at all but a straightforward conflict between traditional and modern schools similar to the struggle that had taken place in nineteenth-century France. When the first public polemics began in the Soviet press between Stalin and Trotsky it so happened that many Communist adherents of the modernist groups in which Russia was then particularly rich, thanks to the efflorescence in all the arts which was the natural outcome of revolutionary fervour, supported Trotsky – not for his political line but because he was known to be sympathetic to their aesthetic principles. One group of modernists actually wrote a letter to *Pravda* in support of Trotsky. The academic painters, eschewing politics entirely as something beyond their ken, remained silent. At this stage Stalin had adopted no position at all on the arts. But when the quarrel with Trotsky became an issue of life and death politically, Stalin identified modern art with those artists who had supported Trotsky and for years they were forgotten men. The academics, who had been more or less politically passive, began to get all the official patronage. In a society without rich men, that meant all the work there was. The modern school was not repressed. For lack of patronage it just went underground. Its practitioners went on painting works which the public never saw. Only after Stalin's death were they seen again, and then only by slow degrees for Khrushchev's personal taste in art was, if anything, even more Victorian than Stalin's. Only in the past two or three years when shrewd collectors such as Ella Winter, the former wife of Lincoln Steffens, returned to Moscow to buy the works of Lissitsky, and when a Canadian Embassy attaché and the Russian wife of Edmund Stevens built up collections in their own houses in Moscow of such artists as Mocx, Galitsin, and Zakharov, have the Soviet authorities become aware that they have been sitting for years on an artistic gold mine whose potential is only just emerging.

Outside the Pushkin we hailed a taxi and asked to be driven to the Savoy Hotel. During the war there had not been a single taxi in the city and only one aged *Intourist* limousine pre-empted for junior diplomats, so the press corps had to travel on foot or in the Metro, but now the sturdy Volga car provides a large taxi fleet at prices rather less than those prevailing in London. The Savoy Hotel, strictly speaking, was no more. In honour of the East German visitors it largely housed it had been renamed the Berlin and the emblem of that city, a large stuffed bear, occupied the place of honour at the door. Paul remembered the hotel from his first visit to Moscow when one could lie in a brass bedstead contemplating a ceiling decorated by Léon Bakst. But when we asked the manageress about those ceilings she sniffed, as though scenting something indelicate, and observed tartly that since we were booked in at the National

the condition of her ceilings fell outside our terms of reference. We formed the impression that she had never heard of Bakst and did not want to get mixed up with such a person at her time of life.

In the foyer we noticed a few West Germans – slender Krupp-type men carrying black briefcases and wearing expensive English shoes. They were in marked contrast with the prevailing East Germans, mostly members of a delegation dominated by an old Lotte Lenya type in a chauffeur's black rubber coat and a proletarian cap set on a cropped head of dyed blonde hair. There was a note of obsequiousness in the East Germans' comments on what they had seen. The GOUM store – *fantastisch, nicht wahr?* – and their souvenirs seemed to consist of plastic toys from the children's store Dietski Mir and balloons with grotesque faces.

But if Paul felt frustrated about the ceilings, the restaurant filled him with delight. It was all and more than we had remembered. The décor is late Victorian French, with ceilings inlaid with mirror glass, elaborate gold scrolls and paintings of nymphs with degenerate Boucher bodies affixed to Victorian faces. There is a fountain and a goldfish pond in the middle of the dance floor. The waiters wear white aprons; the ambiance is faded *Belle Epoque*. Paul whipped out his sketch-book and began to draw the bar, a gilded cornucopia in the midst of which a plump blonde waitress was reflected from a hundred different angles. Apart from foreign delegations with East German and Balkan flags on their tables, there were a number of Russian family parties drinking champagne. Paul ordered chicken à la Kiev – the most delicious practical joke in the world. At the first touch of his fork the butter burst out of its case and shot into his eyes and beard. I should have warned him had I not been too busy with my beef Stroganov which, at eight shillings, was excellent value and very well cooked.

After lunch we drove round the centre of the city, noting the wealth of *art nouveau* architecture in such unexpected places as the Yaroslavsky railway station, the Riabouchinsky house where Gorki used to lodge and the apartment building behind the Bolshoi where many of the dancers live. The Moscow Arts Theatre is, of course, a temple of the period. All four buildings are the work of Shekhtel between 1904 and 1908. They are building a second and larger Arts Theatre which may take precedence over the old building at least for big productions such as *Anna Karenina,* and lest they be tempted to alter the original, Paul got out of the cab and settled down to draw it right away. Central Moscow, which will ultimately be the only old part of the city to be preserved, now divides itself into four clear architectural styles. First, the Empire style in

Moscow: GOUM department store

which the old noblemen's houses in Arbat and along the inner boulevards were built, with their small gardens and coach-houses at the rear. Most of these date from after the Napoleonic holocaust of 1812 but a few, such as the delightful house in which Edmund Stevens lives, remain from the eighteenth century. Second, the *art nouveau* period. Third, a few buildings by Gropius, le Corbusier and their Russian disciples between the wars. Fourth, the Stalin grandiose style, now out of fashion but not out of sight, for a vast amount of building was done in this period – not least, the six or seven late Stalin Gothic skyscrapers which arrest the eye in many sectors.

The largest of these is the new Moscow University, built between 1949 and 1956 on the Lenin Hills from which Napoleon obtained his first view of the Kremlin. The central tower is thirty-four storeys high and the main building alone houses six thousand students. It looks like some mad fancy which even the late William Randolph Hearst could not have willed to happen. Paul's comment was: 'Nothing less like my home town of Cambridge could possibly be imagined.' We walked to the edge of the escarpment where Napoleon is believed to have stood. The view over the city was obscured by mist and this made it easier for me to cast my mind back twenty years when there had been nothing here but a few wooden huts at the end of a dirt road and a ski run which James Aldridge, the novelist, and I had been wont to use to get a good run down onto the frozen river. The run was still there but it had been turned into a permanent jump of Olympic proportions and on the other side of the river were the vast Lenin Stadium and swimming-pool. A double track highway ran through a park surrounding the university towards the Moscow film studios and farther along three or four large new villas stood in wooded gardens. Each had a gatehouse and a broad macadam drive-in. They are the sort of house which an English Midlands industrialist with more money than taste might build for himself and our driver told us: 'Government leaders live there instead of in the Kremlin, where they used to have flats.'

By a fortunate chance we met a solitary walker who turned out to be a British Council exchange student who had been living in the University for ten months. He was obviously an against-the-stream young man who had given up living in London to settle in Scotland where, he said, 'there's still room to lead an open life'. He told us that he lived on 125 roubles* a month plus a grant of ten pounds from the British Council and managed, on this, to save enough to go on holiday trips to the Black Sea or Central Asia, thanks to the low air fares available for students. He lived in a small room high up in the skyscraper and shared a bathroom with one other student,

* At the time we made our journey the exchange rate was 2·5 roubles to the pound sterling.

a Russian. There were, he said, two kitchens on each floor where one could make one's own meals if one wished but the food in the refectory was quite good and cheaper than one could buy and cook oneself. Nevertheless the English students banded together to cook a special dinner each Saturday night. We asked him if it wasn't claustrophobic to live and work in so vast a building.

'In summer, maybe,' he said. 'But in winter it's a damn good idea. You never know what the weather's like outside because it's so well heated. The place may look crazy, but it works. The six thousand of us can lead a complete student life in there and your tutor and all the lecturers are in there with you. At the old Lomonosov building near the Kremlin where four faculties still remain the students live all over town and travel for hours back and forth in freezing weather. We're just pampered, I suppose.'

His view clashed with that of an American woman we met two days later, who told us she had spent a night in a girl student's room there. 'The john kept trickling all night long and the whole place had that odd Russian smell – a mixture of Lysol and just urine, I guess.'

But about his own studies the Englishman was emphatic. He was studying Russian building techniques with a view to writing a thesis and his tutor wanted him to return in a couple of years to supplement his English degree with a Russian one. We asked him the usual silly question and he replied: 'Like it here? Well, I swing between extremes. Sometimes I think this is just about the finest country in the world with the best human beings in it. And then I feel I could scream my head off and go home on the next plane. But about their technique I have few doubts. They had twenty-five million homeless at the end of the war and at the rate they're building now they'll solve their housing problem long before we solve ours. Buildings are going up at the most prodigious rate – all pre-fabricated, of course. With my own eyes I've seen them put up a whole apartment block containing one hundred flats in just thirty days. The standard isn't high – not good enough for our people, I dare say. Though each flat has a good modern kitchen and bathroom, the rooms are too small. The point is – what do people want? Adequate homes quick, or high quality houses ten or twenty years from now? A matter of national temperament, I suppose. But the people here are being given what they want – modern housing just as fast as the industry can do it.'

We asked him about his fellow students and he said, 'You can pick your friends from among every nationality in the Soviet Union and from all over Europe and the Americas as well. The

PaulHOGARTH =SUZdal= Po spaso-Yefimyevsky Monastery

Suzdal: Spasso-Yefimovsky Monastery

Russian girls are very pleasant. Not a bit inhibited. There's no segregation of the sexes, of course. You may have a girl living next door to you – not actually sharing your bathroom, though.'

Driving on to see the Exhibition of Economic Achievement and the monument to Russian astronauts in the north of the city we passed a modest street which testified to the reality of the 'thaw'. It was named after Marshal Tukhachevsky, one of the most distinguished victims of the pre-war purge of the Red Army.

We went, still drawn by the image of *art nouveau*, to have dinner at the Metropole. The domed restaurant here, about the size of the old Carlton in the Haymarket, was in its heyday just before the first World War. It enjoyed a scandalous reputation, rather like Romano's in the Strand, but Romanov's would have been a better name for it because it was the haunt of officers of the Imperial Army, who found its location on Theatre Square very convenient for entertaining the corps de ballet of the Bolshoi. Officers would take a suite in the hotel and many a dancer must have found her way upstairs past my chaste statue of liberty after having champagne drunk from her slipper in the restaurant. I recognized some of the waiters from the war years, when the restaurant was closed because of the danger of the glass roof falling in; many were grandfathers who had worked in the hotel since before the revolution. Paul and I had a good bortsch, a steak and cheese for £1 a head. The Georgian red wine was not cheap at 25s. a bottle but it was passable.

Next morning snow still lay thick in the Alexandrovsky Garden beneath the Kremlin Wall but the sun was shining and our spirits rose when one of the managers of *Intourist* arrived to plan our itinerary with us. His name was Kulikov. He had a sharp Nordic physiognomy not unlike the young Hans Andersen and observed in a quizzical manner, by way of introduction: 'Mine is a curious name – it is really *kulik,* a small marsh fowl.' At once one could imagine him onomatopoeically crying: 'Kuleek! Kuleek!' as he picked a delicate path across some desolate fen. Our travel plans sounded all right as we ran through them but despite another long session at the telephone with Kulikov to assist me it proved impossible to reach more than one of our contacts – whom we gratefully snapped up for an evening at the theatre – and we had visions of arriving at some distant point in Central Asia without anyone being aware of our presence or showing the least interest in what we were seeking to do.

Meanwhile an opportunity arose for me to lose myself once again in a big Moscow crowd and to speculate about why it is that, although I have never been able to identify myself with the Russian people but only with the experiment they have been absorbed in these past fifty years,

I have always felt at home in Moscow, as though I had lived there in some previous existence and owed a debt of loyalty to the very stones of the place. Red flags with black borders were hanging from all the buildings around the Kremlin. A State Funeral was in the making for Marshal Malinovsky, the Defence Minister, and the crowds which were assembling seemed very much a throw-back to the war years. A good many peasants had come up from the country for the occasion, many of them with war medals pinned on their thick winter coats. There were a lot of country women in big black boots and a great many of those maidenly young Russians who scorn fashionable clothing but spend their money on sensible furs and perhaps a silk kerchief to bind up their hair. Despite the cold, the ice-cream sellers were doing a brisk trade and a few gypsy families were wandering through the crowd selling single flowers sealed up in cellophane packets to protect them from the icy wind. At this time of year flowers are so rare and so costly that a Moscow girl is quite happy to accept a single flower from her boy friend where a girl in the more temperate West would be insulted by anything less than a bunch or a posy.

I could detect no signs of bourgeois degeneracy among this crowd. A little better dressed than in the war years, certainly, but still basically sporting that working-class uniform of sober woollens and thick leather which Stalin and Mao Tse-tung, each in his own way, had made obligatory for all true followers of Lenin. Kosygin himself is a well-dressed man but most of the faithful still seem to dress themselves in the sort of unpressed, hard-wearing garments that go with high thinking and low living – the sort which Lenin and his wife Krupskaya wore, whether in Russia or abroad, through all their years together. Paul suggested that the older generation of party stalwarts deliberately make themselves look dowdy as a protest against those whose tendency towards elegant dress may be thought to indicate a deviationist political line. And of course it is true that smart young Russians with little interest in the political thinking of their elders are not likely to be found at the funeral of an old marshal who had died of cancer after winning his glory before they were born.

Still, they were a well-mannered, easy-going crowd. The only individual who got out of hand was a small urchin who climbed on the roof of the Metro station to get a better view and then unscrewed the electric strip lighting shaped into an 'M' and made off with it, a sizable souvenir almost as large as himself. No one tried to stop the thief and if any militia-man saw what had happened he gave no sign. Perhaps he thought it would be 'uncultured' to arrest a small boy during a state funeral.

Presently thousands of civilians moved in columns twenty abreast into the square, carrying black-bordered photographs of the dead man, and took up their places opposite the Mausoleum. The coffin was borne into the square on a rocket-carrier towed behind an amphibious armoured vehicle with the insignia of a Guards division painted on it. Troops from this same division provided the guard of honour. They marched with that stamping Russian quick-step which draws electric sparks from the paving-stones, the men swinging their arms across the body, the officers swinging their arms fore and aft as in a gymnastic display, with a drawn sabre couched between wrist and shoulder. There were murmurs of approval from old soldiers in the crowd as the guard swung past; one old man called out 'beautiful; well done!' Two bands were mounted in the square and only desisted from funereal music while the speeches were being delivered from the rostrum. Finally the leaders of the party and government stepped down from the tomb and carried the ashes, buried among flowers, out of our sight to the Kremlin wall where they were laid behind a modest plaque.

After the mourners had dispersed I joined a queue which had formed to look at the wreaths. We snaked along the Kremlin wall, past the black marble plaques which honour the old Marxists, some of them foreign, who died in Russia and were actually buried there. Communist leaders who are buried abroad are not honoured in this way. The plaques date back to 1924. Directly behind the Lenin mausoleum is the plaque to his wife. There too are six full-length graves of black marble such as you might find in an English churchyard. They form part of the plinth of the mausoleum itself. The first five belong to Kalinin, Sverdlov, Dzerzkinsky, Zhdanov and Frunze and they carry busts in the same style but the sixth grave has no bust and the lettering on it has not been gilded. It says merely *J. V. Stalin*, with the date of his birth and death. I had wrongly assumed that when Stalin was removed from the Lenin mausoleum he had been interred in the wall with the others, but this is not so. He occupies a place of conspicuous honour, despite all the denunciations that have been made against his record. The grave is unfinished and yet it must presumably be finished one day, or else the symmetry of this special graveyard will be destroyed. It was quite obvious that the queue was slowing down as this grave was reached. Few people near me made any comment but all regarded it with close attention. Two old country women behind me halted before it, ignoring the nudges of those behind them. One sighed and said: 'Oh dear, it is a pity.' Evidently she was referring to the condition of the grave. The other said cryptically: 'Yes, but you must remember the moral issue.'

Indeed, and the moral issue is highly complex. Stalin has been dead a long while and a generation is growing up which rarely thinks of him. But his ghost will not lie down and the historians are plagued by his memory. The new *Short History of the USSR* (published in Moscow in English in 1965) attempts to put the Stalin period in perspective but no one who lived through that period could possibly be convinced by its timid assertions. In two lavishly illustrated volumes not a single picture of Stalin appears and he is represented as a sort of committee chairman who erred through not taking his colleagues into his confidence. There are no quotations from Stalin's major speeches and even Khrushchev's speech denouncing Stalin's errors at the 20th Congress of the party is skated over. The authors merely say: 'The Central Committee exposed the gross violations of socialist legality and abuses of power that occurred in Stalin's time and decided to tell the people about them . . . though it knew this might create bitterness, even some discontent. It knew too that its candid criticism of errors might be used by enemies for anti-Soviet ends . . . While criticizing the errors and distortions made by Stalin, the party gave him due credit for his previous services to the country and the international working-class movement.' Fair enough, one might think, in a short historical summary. But this history, in seeking to re-attribute to Lenin most of the glory wrongly appropriated by Stalin, burkes the awkward fact that Lenin – due to the lingering illness which followed the attempt to assassinate him – was in effective control of the Soviet State for little more than four years while, during the ensuing thirty years in which the Soviet Union rose from the condition of an economically backward, illiterate peasant society which it still was in the year of Lenin's death, to become the second power in the world, the man at the helm was Joseph Stalin. How, one asks oneself, if Stalin's errors and misdemeanours were as deep-seated and fundamental as Khrushchev declared them to be, was it possible that this faulty helmsman could have brought the ship of state so triumphantly to port? To this the Khrushchevites would reply: it was done *despite Stalin* thanks to the great qualities of the Russian people. It is true that even had the Central Committee decided against revealing Stalin's errors when they did, the veneration of his person had reached such an absurd pitch after the war that there must sooner or later have been a reaction against it. I take no pride in my record as a Kremlinologist but in an article written for the *Daily Express* over twenty years ago I answered the question 'What do you dislike most in Russia?' in this wise:

Stalin-worship – unworthy throw-back to that 'old Oriental backwardness' which both Lenin and Stalin spent their lives in fighting and which, Stalin himself says, 'grates unpleasantly on the ear'.

The real veneration in which Stalin is held is cheapened by sycophancy in almost every public speech. Recently, in the Supreme Soviet, someone spoke of Stalin as the 'genius-coryphée at the head of Soviet science'. Had Stalin been there, he probably would have burst out laughing. As he was not, every face assumed a Sunday School look, each pair of hands applauded.

Nevertheless, the opening-up of the Kremlin shortly after Stalin's death must be seen as an act of great symbolic significance. It marked the beginning of a new era. Even in Lenin's day, the Kremlin was a closely guarded place and in the Stalin period it was completely inaccessible to ordinary people. During my four years in Russia I entered it only twice, to attend meetings of the Supreme Soviet and to look over the treasures in the Armoury. Stalin made the Kremlin a symbol of statecraft known throughout the world but it was also a fortress presided over by a genius, or an ogre, depending on how you saw him. Stalin lived and worked there. Those who knew where to look could see his lights burning all night. Nor was there anything new in this immolation of State power within the fortress. For hundreds of years the Kremlin was closed to all but the Rulers and the clergy though it had always been holy ground to the Russian people. The founder of Moscow, Yuri Dolgoruky, chose this piece of high ground at the confluence of rivers to be his strong place and where the waters did not flow he built a moat so as to isolate the Kremlin completely from the land. His followers first pitched their tents in a circle around the fort and then began to build permanent structures of wood in an ever-widening circle around it. Under the latest plan for the reconstruction of Moscow, all the main avenues lead to the Kremlin, like the spokes of a wheel. The magnificent churches and palaces, the arsenal and parade ground which grew up within the Kremlin became, as the Russian state extended its power, a temple and a symbol of the tribe very much as the temple at Jerusalem became an embodiment of Jewish unity and Jewish uniqueness. In the nineteenth century the Slavophiles aspired to make Moscow 'the new Jerusalem', the centre of a Slav power which was to be purer and less materialistic than Rome though it was to have the same universality. And the Kremlin was to be the centre of their faith. How this aspiration was to a large extent realized under Stalin after he had defeated the internationalism of Trotsky in order to 'build socialism in one country', even though this ran counter to the messianic conception of the Jewish founder of Marxism and was indubitably anathema to many of the Jews – besides Trotsky – who had played so large a part in establishing the international Communist movement, and how the success of Stalin's policy set up tensions between the victorious Russian school of Communists and the supra-national school to which many Jews adhered – all this requires more space to elaborate than I possess. But I shall return to it later when I discuss the present situation of Russian Jewry because I believe it plays a considerable part in that situation.

When the Kremlin gates were opened and the populace surged in, it was not enough to let them roam around the palaces and churches and enjoy the wind-swept air of its terraces, which a Scot might compare with Edinburgh Castle. The old Kremlin Theatre was opened to visiting theatrical companies and the Palace of Congresses was built not only to provide a six-thousand seat auditorium for conferences but also as a new *filial* for the Bolshoi Theatre. A pleasant young man from the USSR–Great Britain Society named Shirayev took Paul and me to hear the Bolshoi company do *Carmen*. We sat in the director's box and not a seat in the auditorium was empty. The Kremlin Theatre was also full that night, which meant that at least eight thousand people had passed through the narrow Troitsky or Spassky gates. The acoustics were good and the production lavish but although one could hear each word of recitative one could scarcely see the singers' faces and the production was so vast that the modest square in Seville looked like Times Square in the rush hour. We left after the third act, suffering from cultural indigestion. Yet it had been a most impressive evening. Shirayev told us that most of his friends had been horrified at first at the idea of erecting a large modern building in the Kremlin, even though the architectural spectrum there already covers many centuries. But in the long run they had become reconciled. The Palace has been sunk several storeys into the ground so that it does not tower over the Kremlin battlements. The finish of the building is immaculate, both inside and out, and the décor is in excellent taste. At the point where the Palace is joined onto the medieval Kremlin palace the architects have provided a winter garden filled with orange trees and tropical plants arranged around a fountain. 'It's fun to come up here when the snow is falling', said Shirayev, 'and luxuriate in all this warmth.'

The top floor of the Palace is reached by a system of moving stairways. Here a huge ballroom runs the full length of the building and, in the long intervals that Russian audiences love, there is provision for six thousand people to have supper. One of the Tsars once gave a ball for six thousand guests and this ballroom mirrors the same imperial grandeur. Dozens of tables draped in spotless linen serve *bliny* and caviare, mushrooms in cream, sausage and ham in open sandwiches, beer, wines and champagne and the delicious Russian ices made from real cream. The scene resembles a coronation banquet except that the guests are in lounge suits or simple dresses.

'My God, the biggest nosh-up in the world', said an awed English voice behind me. If one built a palace like this for the English people within some royal enclave such as Windsor, one can imagine the holocaust of cigarette ends and bits of paper they would leave behind! But this place was spotless. Separate chambers are reserved for those who wish to smoke. Again, if one permitted an English architect of the dominant concrete box school to build a modern palace physically linked with Windsor Castle, what would the ensemble look like? The mind shrinks from contemplating such a prospect: one evades the issue by rejoining that in England such a synthesis would never be attempted.

The next building which Paul sat down to draw while I was engaged inside was a very old friend of mine – the Edwardian rococo building in Prospekt Kalinina which was one of thirty mansions in the city that had once belonged to the collector of post-impressionists, Morozov. Just before we were due there I telephoned a number which Tom Driberg, M.P. had given me. It was that of Archie Johnstone, who had been editor of *Britansky Soyuznik,* the Russian weekly which the British Ministry of Information used to issue in Moscow until he became disillusioned by Ernest Bevin's foreign policy after the war and decided to stay on in Moscow and marry a Russian girl. The Morozov mansion had been his headquarters: part of it was used as a British club, and as such it appears in my novel, *Two Ways in the World*, under the guise of the British Cultural Mission. But when I got Mrs. Johnstone on the phone she told me that her husband had died three years before. This was melancholy news because it reinforced the feeling I had long had that those few Englishmen who had sacrificed their future by remaining in Moscow, not out of any overpowering sense of commitment but through the inanition of despair, had sacrificed themselves in vain.

Another such was Ralph Parker, *The Times* correspondent who had appeared a veritable pillar of the establishment with his cosy dinners for the British Ambassador at his flat in Koklovsky Pereulok but who had gone to the *News Chronicle* and then to the *Daily Worker* out of a growing sense of outrage over British policy, and had died in Russia just before the Cold War had started to fade. These men had nothing in common with the renegade diplomats Burgess and Maclean, or with Kim Philby. They were dissenters of the same calibre as the pro-Boers at the beginning of the century, but while a pro-Boer like Lloyd George could carry his bat through the bad years and become Prime Minister and a national hero, the Cold War exacted a savage retribution against those who elected to sit it out on the other side of the hill. They were branded as traitors although they had neither the opportunity nor the desire to commit an act of treachery and the mere circumstance of continuing to live in Russia without any British connection was held against them.

Johnstone's old workplace was now 'Friendship House', the headquarters of the Soviet society for cultural relations with foreign countries. I was hospitably received there by officials of the USSR–Great Britain Society. They showed me an exhibition of paintings by the Siberian artist Gritchuk and I showed them the marble hall where James Aldridge and I had played the first game of badminton ever seen in Moscow with a set I had bought while on leave in Cairo. When I finally left Moscow I handed the equipment over to Johnstone's Russian staff, who spread knowledge of the game among their friends. Badminton is the ideal game for a country with a severe climate because it can be played indoors all the year round. Eventually Khrushchev took up the game at his holiday villa on the Black Sea and in the Army and Navy Stores a few doors down the street I had been pleased to see a whole window full of badminton sets. As we went round the fantastic rooms of the mansion my hosts asked me if I had seen anything so odd before. The answer was that its *nouveau riche* splendours reminded me of Sir Philip Sassoon's mansion in Park Lane, since pulled down to make way for the American Bunny Club.

When Paul had finished work on 'Friendship House' we went to lunch with Nesterov, the secretary of the USSR–Great Britain Society, and some of his assistants. Nesterov is a well-groomed youngish man whose English, after three years in the London embassy, is excellent. He has a mild, intellectual's face. Indeed, he could be one of those progressive parsons which the Church of England now produces whose loosely based Christianity would have been accounted atheism a generation ago – the kind of cleric who, you feel, would appeal to Harold Wilson as a future Bishop of Winchester. But beneath Nesterov's easy manners one could detect the outline of a strong party man. Our conversation touched on the danger – as I expressed it – of harking back too much to the war in compiling this book. Paul said his students at the Royal College of Art are heartily sick of war reminiscences. What interest would one have at twenty-one in a war that had ended before one was born? But Nesterov had not forgotten the war, though he was only ten when it ended.

'You can't get modern Russia in perspective at all,' he said, 'if you forget that we lost twenty million dead and that twenty-five millions were left without homes. A disaster of such magnitude is not forgotten in twenty years.'

And he told us how, two days before the war began, he was taken to Kiev by his mother on holiday. When the news came that the Germans had crossed the frontier no one believed it. Only when retreating Russian soldiers straggled into Kiev did it seem real. And then everything was in chaos. He and his mother moved back with the retreating army on foot, sometimes being given a ride in a truck, all the way to Moscow. Here his mother vowed to retreat no farther. Their flat was in a western suburb and at night they could see the red glow at the front and the flashes of the guns twenty miles away. The Germans actually got to within fifteen miles of the Kremlin before they drew back. Boys such as he, with no schools to go to, were organized by the Komsomol to go down to the frozen river each morning and pick up the fragments of ack-ack shells that had fallen on the ice the night before. They were collected for scrap and sent to the factories.

I looked at this smooth young executive who seems likely to go far in the foreign service. As though reading my thoughts, he said: 'I have an interesting life today. But, you see, like millions of other kids who survived, I had a hard childhood.'

We got round to the subject of China and Nesterov and his colleagues seemed as nonplussed as we were. 'It all makes no sense,' they said. China had been making rapid progress; she would soon have been a great power in fact as well as in name but for the sake of a mad ideological whim she had thrown all this away and found herself with scarcely a friend left in the world. They hoped that in time the Chinese Communist Party would rally its forces and set China back on the right road. Meanwhile they conceived Mao Tse-tung to be the evil genius of the situation. His famous 'Let a hundred flowers bloom, let a hundred modes of thought contend' was very far, they thought, from being a liberal gesture. On the contrary, it was a poet's device to identify his enemies.

'When the hundred flowers *did* come up and bloom, Mao quietly lopped off their heads.'

Our luncheon was one of those timeless Russian ones which can so easily extend themselves past tea-time into the evening hours but Paul and I had a busy afternoon ahead of us so that, in the event, we spent little more time at table than the English business man habitually does.

We rushed back to the hotel to record an interview for Moscow Radio that evening and then went to the offices of the magazine *Foreign Literature* for a meeting with Sava Dangulov, its assistant editor. Dangulov had been in the Foreign Office during the war and had been my conducting officer on trips to the front. He is also a poet and a novelist and had visited me in

Moscow: Art Nouveau apartment house

London the year before while he was collecting material for a novel dealing with the Marxist exiles who lived in England before the revolution. He went to the principal haunts of Marx and Lenin in Clerkenwell, Highgate and Bloomsbury and asked me for introductions to such period figures as Sir Robert Bruce Lockhart and Baroness Budberg. He managed in three weeks to fill several notebooks and at the end had only one ambition unfulfilled.

'There is one place I haven't succeeded in getting into,' he said. 'Could you help me?'

'Of course. What is it?'

'Brixton Prison.'

Alas, I did not know the Governor of Brixton or any of his guests at this time, so I was unable to help. But I had little doubt that Dangulov, who used to be known among the correspondents as 'the dashing Circassian' because of the gallant way he turned a phrase – 'Ah, how she radiates moral purity!' he once found it possible to say about one unprepossessing female journalist – would get himself inside if anyone could.

The meeting he had arranged this afternoon proved to be profoundly soothing and flattering for two individuals such as ourselves, long accustomed to the low esteem in which artists and writers are held in England. Almost the entire staff of the magazine were waiting for us in a book-lined room around a table set with cakes, coffee cups and those lush Russian chocolates which come wrapped in flower-decked paper. We sat down to a sort of *conversazione* during which a photographer moved around us taking pictures from every angle and a stenographer took down the exchanges so that they might be edited and appear later as a feature in the magazine. Paul spoke about his work as a tutor of drawing at the Royal College of Art and about the extraordinary renascence taking place in the fine arts among the new generation of students, largely from working-class families, who had never been exposed to an art education before. His conclusions were optimistic. Mine could not be. I spoke about the sorry situation of English writers in an economy which forces all but a few to work full-time at other jobs because the rewards of literature are so low. And I dwelt on the Society of Authors' plan, so well advocated by Sir Alan Herbert, to provide a small additional income for authors by means of a levy on books borrowed from public libraries. We then faced a rain of questions about every conceivable aspect of painting and writing in England. Dangulov led the conversation without dominating it and encouraged his staff to join in. We could not have been more politely listened to had we been two eminent members of the *Académie Française*. The leisurely talk, the serene atmosphere of this former nobleman's house in Pyatnitskaya Ulitsa with the trees struggling to emerge from the sodden snow outside the french windows, the touchingly simple faith in the value of all creative struggle, the complete absence of cynicism – all this pointed to the continued existence in Russia of that sheer love of mental exercise which we find in Turgeniev and Tolstoy. Such talk might perhaps have been paralleled in the Bloomsbury of Virginia Woolf and Lytton Strachey; it might have been heard forty years ago in Florence when Aldous Huxley and D. H. Lawrence met in exile but I don't believe it could have been attempted in modern London. We are so afraid of appearing pretentious nowadays that conversation rarely gets off the ground at all. Even the Royal Society of Literature meets so seldom and its members have so little to say to one another when they do that they might as well not meet at all.

Dangulov and his staff, in their turn, seemed diffident about their own work. With all foreign literature to choose from, how could one be sure one was making the best selection every quarter? And how much good work in little-known languages was getting clean away?

It seemed to me that a society in which it is possible to print four hundred thousand copies of a magazine which deals in nothing but the work of foreigners should inspire its members with confidence. And lest it be thought that Russian intellectuals rush to buy Dangulov's journal because the indigenous magazines are filled with the work of party hacks, it should be remembered that *Liternaturnaya Gazeta* sells two million copies each week. True, there is much justified dissatisfaction about the restrictive policies of the old guard of the Writers Union and the Union of Artists and about the stranglehold which the Moscow Arts Theatre and the Maly still exert upon theatrical taste, but when it comes to respect for and encouragement of the archetypal business of arranging words in good order upon paper, we could take a course from the Russians – and a post-graduate course as well.

★　　★　　★

When the sun went down we were faced with a dreary evening of slanting sleet and overflowing pavements. Paul wanted to try the restored Praga Restaurant which had been strongly recommended by John Gunter in *Inside Russia*, but there were no taxis to be had. The only vehicle in sight was a cab already occupied by a young woman. She was seated next to the driver, a massive fellow with an enormous tweed headpiece which in my school days had been called a 'tout cap' but which, because of its large flat surface, is known to Russians as an 'aerodrome', and very popular it is, too, among Armenians and Georgians. The young woman kept looking over her shoulder as though waiting for some companions to come out of the hotel and get in at the back. I stood at the kerb trying, without success, to flag passing vehicles. And then I noticed the woman making signals to indicate we might share the cab with her. Paul and I ran through the slush and got in. The driver presented an impassive back to us and said no word. The negotiations were conducted by the young woman who said it would be no trouble to drop us off at the Praga. As she turned round to speak to us I saw that she had the bright excited eyes you see in some gypsy women, the sort of eyes that used to go with consumption in the days when it was a fatal disease. She possessed the acute, dirty loveliness that goes with a dauntless heart and slovenly habits and I thought at once of those tawdry heroines of Dostoevsky. Over her shoulder she smiled at Paul and me as though extending to us an equal measure of tolerance and contempt. She said to me: 'Are you a Finn?' and when I said I was an Englishman she turned away as though this nationality held no interest for her. The taxi driver did not seem to know the way and he had not switched on his meter but she directed him and when we stopped at the restaurant and I asked how much we owed, she shrugged her shoulders and said: 'Nothing.' I pressed my point, as politeness demanded, and she said: 'Ah, it's only a beginning.' Her friend the driver still did not show us his face. As I again waggled my wallet at her, she said: 'Well, if you insist – one rouble.' The proper fare would have been forty kopecks, less than half. And then the significance of 'It's only a beginning' dawned on me. This wild creature was 'on the game'. The taxi driver was her protector and the ploy outside the hotel a means of selecting likely customers without committing oneself prematurely or giving the police an excuse to pounce.

My day in Moscow had been the day of the enthusiastic amateur, especially the self-styled student of languages. Prostitution was impracticable because no rooms were available and no meeting places open. The Cocktail Hall in Gorki Street – now a tea room – was then the only place where public drinking could be indulged in, the customers were rationed to three drinks and there was always a queue waiting to get in. But now that Moscow is full of foreign business men and tourists the old Adam may have to be catered for in the traditional way. The authorities cannot do it and would not if they could. The oldest profession is the only one which cannot be nationalized and so the field seems to be open for private enterprise.

The Praga was a disappointment to Paul though not to me, for there had been nothing like it

National Hotel, Moscow

in my day. A long building with a cupola at each end, it resembles a popular restaurant in Stockholm deriving from some distant Parisian prototype. A number of restaurants are linked around a central kitchen. The décor of each varies but the food is the same. I would have settled for the Praga, but Paul, in perfectionist mood, wanted something more typically Muscovite. So we found an ordinary taxi without a pretty gypsy in the front seat and made the rounds. Alone among great cities, Moscow does not possess a single foreign restaurant. There is no French, Italian, Chinese or Indian food to be had, except within the embassies. The reason is that if a restaurateur from abroad were allowed to set up his own establishment – for few chefs of quality would agree to serve merely as an official of the Soviet Ministry of Food – then the Ministry's elaborate network would be undermined and the right to profit from the labour of others which is barred by the constitution would be extended to foreigners. Those who want exotic fare have to content themselves with Georgian, Armenian or Uzbek restaurants, which exist in all the main cities. But the number of restaurants available has not kept pace with the rise in the standard of living, as we quickly found out.

We went first to the Aragvi, the only restaurant to remain open in Moscow all through the war whose Georgian cuisine is excellent by any reckoning, and found a long queue waiting to get in. An important-looking gentleman carrying a brief-case went to the head of the queue amid angry muttering from those at the back and after a lot of argument was able to convince the doorman that he was the guest of someone who had already booked a table. He got in, but Paul and I were turned away. A few years before, our foreign status would have secured us admission ahead of any Russian and I could not but think that the withdrawal of privilege was right. We then joined the queue outside a neighbouring Armenian restaurant with the same result and were turned away from the Berlin, which had been taken over for the evening by some sportsmen's club.

We passed a number of cafés and small eating-houses whose windows were steamed over with the mass of clients within. Tightening our coat collars against the driving sleet and lowering our standards, we made for the restaurant of the Moskva Hotel. Here we were able to share a table with a couple of Rumanian tourists with whom, rather to our relief, we were unable to exchange a word in a common language. The atmosphere was rather like that of a Lyons Corner House. Waitresses were in charge and there was an all-girl band. The Moskva, built in 1936, was redecorated after the war. Green marble pillars at least sixty feet high support a ceiling which has been painted with an impression of the victory salute in Moscow in 1945. The restaurant appears to be as long as the Galerie des Glaces at Versailles. But notwithstanding these oppressive surroundings, the food was good. We had a fine Russian salad, a passable steak, a sufficiency of vodka, a bottle of Soviet champagne and a Georgian brandy for £2 5s. a head.

'You seem depressed,' said Paul. 'Visually, Moscow is an artist's gold mine but of course you have to dig beneath the surface. It's more difficult for you. What are your impressions so far?'

I searched for a comprehensive answer but could not find one.

'I'm a little disappointed. I haven't any right to be. My disappointment springs from a thoroughly silly reason. Still, I feel it.'

'You mean, things have changed, and not for the better?'

'Oh, entirely for the better. But when I first came here – nearly a quarter of a century ago – the Germans were just forty miles from Moscow. You remember what Dr. Johnson said about how wonderfully the mind is clarified when one knows one is to be hanged on the morrow? Everything was clear here in those days and though many people were nearly starving, the atmosphere was bright. These people were fighting for their lives, and our lives too. The fate of the world depended on what happened at the front a few miles from here. Well, the heroic tension that enveloped Moscow in those days has quite gone. Moscow looks like any other great city – on the surface. The great days are long past. People are living their disparate lives again. It's natural, and quite right. It is not war and it isn't magnificent. Once it was both. There were only a handful of West Europeans here in those days and we few will never forget them.'

Paul pulled an indignant face. 'I hope you're not going to tell me,' he said, 'that Stalin won the war.'

'No. As Stalin was the first to admit, the Russian people won the war. The German Army was beaten here, as Churchill too conceded – not in Western Europe. And beaten by Russian arms – not by Lease-Lend donations. But nobody questioned Stalin's leadership then, least of all Khrushchev. If you had seen Stalin and Khrushchev together, as I have done, if you had seen the look of utter devotion which Khrushchev gave the old man, you'd have had as much difficulty as I did in swallowing Khrushchev's denunciation of him four years after he was dead. That's not to say that many of the charges against Stalin were not perfectly true. He was not a good man. Good men are relatively common. He was a great man, a world changer of the calibre of Caesar, Cromwell and Napoleon and, like them, despite all the blunders and crimes he committed, he was capable of binding men to him with hoops of steel.'

'A man of steel, certainly – he chose the name for himself. But Lenin was loved and, if he had lived, the steely one could have gone back to calling himself Djugashvili because we would probably never have heard of him. Lenin would have got rid of him. We know that from Lenin's testament.'

'Perhaps. But if men died because of Stalin, they also died for him. I've seen the letter which my old friend Olga Hludova received from her brother Mitya at the front. Alexander Werth quotes it in his book – and rightly, because it typifies the atmosphere of that time.'

I quoted as much of the letter as I could remember:

I've been proposed for the Patriotic War Order and, better still, I've been accepted into the Party. Yes, I know my father and mother were bourgeois, but what the hell! I'm a Russian, 100%, and proud of it, and our people have made this victory possible, after all the terror and humiliation of 1941: and I am ready to give my life for my country and for Stalin. I am proud to be in the Party, to be one of Stalin's victorious soldiers. If I'm lucky enough I'll be in Berlin yet. We'll get there – and we deserve to get there – before our Western Allies do.

'Mitya was only nineteen when he wrote that letter, early in 1944. A week later he was dead.'

'Very moving,' said Paul. 'But people can't live at that level all their lives, and nor can nations.'

'I entirely agree. That's why I *know* my disappointment is irrational. When Lincoln Steffens led the Western influx here, forty years ago, Russia, for most people, was just a bad joke, a bad smell. Now she's the second most developed country in the world, and potentially the greatest, and I'm glad I lived through the Stalin period when all this was happening. Stalin may have been an ogre, but he was an ogre of genius. In his time one lived dangerously, but it was exhilarating. His successors have been able men but they are not in the same class. They are just politicians. And to my eye the people are beginning to assume the lack-lustre look of people who *know* they are governed by politicians – machine politicians at that – and are not very happy about it because they've been used to something better.'

'Better? with labour camps and arrests in the night?'

'Oh yes, much better, and more principled too. Isn't it always better to travel than to arrive? The Communist Party of the Soviet Union has become the most successful, the most respected and respectable of established bodies. But once, when it had the world to win, it was the Church Militant, in whose service millions were prepared to sacrifice everything.'

'What you really mean,' said Paul, 'is that the Russians are beginning to look like us.'

'I wouldn't wish that on anyone. When I was born a quarter of the globe was painted red and the English believed in their destiny. Now we are an uncommitted and uncertain people. Still, I ought not to make snap judgments after so short a period of re-acquaintance. Let's push on to Suzdal, Samarkand, Bukhara, Tashkent, Tbilisi, Kiev and Leningrad and not attempt to sum up for at least another month.'

Moscow: The Historic Tower

3 SUZDAL

'The train for Suzdal, via Vladimir, leaves at three p.m.,' said the *Intourist* woman.

'We were told there was a morning train,' said Paul. 'You see, if we leave in the afternoon and the journey takes three hours, we'll waste a whole day there and our time is very short.'

'I am sorry. There is only one train a day.'

'Vladimir is on the main line to Gorki,' I said. 'Surely there must be more than one train?'

'Only one.'

'Tell her the train's no use. We'll hire a car and go first thing in the morning,' said Paul.

I did so. But the indomitable woman, who looked like a retired German governess who had taken the job for pin money and plainly did not like it, sensed that I did not believe her and her pale puffy cheeks began to glow.

'It is forbidden to go by road.'

'Why then does *Intourist* produce a guide-book which says – *a pleasant drive by bus of less than two hours on the Gorki highway brings you to Vladimir?*'

'The road is indeed pleasant. But it is not open to foreigners.'

'Rubbish,' said I.

'Please not to call me rubbish. I am only an employee who is doing her best – you cannot blame me for the regulations of *Intourist* or the rules of our government.'

'Are you telling me the Soviet Government forbids me to travel to Vladimir in a Soviet bus?'

The *Intourist* woman was now as scarlet as a Kremlin star. 'I am telling you our government provides a comfortable train for you to travel in. Please take it.'

'Very well. But a morning train.'

'You are wasting my time. I've already told you there is none.'

I felt myself becoming as angry as she was. 'How many souls live in Gorki?'

'I do not know.'

'One million. And you expect me to believe there is only one train a day to so great a city?'

The woman was, of course, lying. It turned out to be one of those idiotic polite lies one meets with in the Soviet Union which earn contempt because they are so unnecessary. Paul was alarmed by the inscription on the tickets. It said 'Hard Class' and I, recalling an earlier journey between Molotovsk on the White Sea and Archangel in unheated carriages in the depth of winter, spoke up in favour of austerity. But we need not have worried. 'Hard' proved to be an electric train made up of modern coaches with airplane-type reclining seats with foam-rubber upholstery and folding tables for each passenger. There was a buffet instead of the old-style samovar in each carriage and the train gave us as comfortable a second-class journey as we had ever enjoyed. The conductor told us the train went down to Vladimir, a distance of 120 miles, each afternoon and came back to Moscow early the next morning. 'You are lucky,' he said. 'The other trains on this line are the old "hard" stock.'

'All is explained!' said I to Paul. 'This is a Potemkin train – like the artificial cottages and spotless peasants which Potemkin arranged to charm Catherine the Great when she toured the provinces so that she wouldn't see the true squalor of Russia. It's far from being the only train but it's the only one *Intourist* wants us to see.'

The train ran express for the first forty miles out of the Kursk station and then stopped at country stations all the way to Vladimir, picking up and setting down peasant families, each of whom had booked their seats on the Potemkin special. The suburbs of Moscow seemed almost as endless as London's but eventually the factories and apartment blocks under construction gave way to wooden houses, and when the real country came it was a rolling plain with thick forest land interspersed with collective farms. The unpainted wooden shacks weren't pretty to look at but I knew their warmth and relative spaciousness from experience. They all had electricity and TV aerials sprouted on almost every roof. Between the villages there was a great sense of space – a sense of rivers to fish in, forest tracks to walk along, a sense of belonging to a wider world than

Suzdal: Rozhdestvensky Cathedral

any we in Western Europe know, a world where nothing is fenced in. Standing alone on the boundless plain under the vast open sky one becomes aware of the risks inherent in the possession of so much land which must be coveted by many less fortunate people across the distant frontiers. The historic sacrifice of holding Mongols, Tartars and Turks at bay while at the same time being stabbed in the back by the ungrateful Christian West, of fighting Teutonic knights, Swedish barons and Polish Catholic crusaders at the same time as one was keeping the most savage enemies of these fellow-Christians away from the frontiers of Europe – no wonder such an experience has left scars on the Russian mind.

We reached Vladimir at six o'clock of a warm evening. On the escarpment above the railway station stands the white-walled Kremlin with the Uspensky Cathedral at its highest point. Long before Moscow was built the cathedral was the seat of the Patriarch of All Russia when the principality of Vladimir–Suzdal was the capital of the Russian state in the twelfth century. From the terrace of the cathedral, which is a 'live' one, one can see for miles to the south and west where the river Klyazma meanders across the plain. Around the cathedral gardens have been laid out and here thousands of townsfolk were promenading, as in a Spanish town. We joined the promenaders and after a while an old woman with her grandson came up and said to Paul: 'My little fellow here has just said – "Look at Lenin over there!" meaning you' and, indicating Paul's beard, she roared with laughter.

At the centre of the garden is the statue of Yuri Dolgoruky, who went from Vladimir to found Moscow in the twelfth century. And on a classical eighteenth-century building close by there is a plaque inscribed in English:

Vladimir special English Language School: no. 23
run by the RSFSR Ministry of Education.

Here education is entirely in English from junior school to graduation – a new development in the USSR which seems to owe something to the success of the French Lycées in foreign countries, though these schools are completely indigenous.

At the modest Vladimir Hotel it became apparent that we were the only foreigners in this city of 150,000 people for we were invited to ignore the menu and order whatever we fancied for dinner. We vaguely suggested some bortsch and perhaps a steak. On arrival in the dining-room where a Union Jack was stuck on our table we were given cold fat bacon served with horseradish sauce followed by the best bortsch I had yet eaten in Russia. It contained black olives as well as the traditional ingredients. Next came two earthenware pots which were found to contain steak in a rich sauce of mushrooms, hard-boiled eggs, onions and green peppers topped off with a layer of pastry. With this delicious dish we drank vodka, a Russian Riesling, Georgian brandy and coffee and the bill came to £1 16s. a head. The hotel rooms were depressing at first sight but the dining-room is in a new wing facing the river and a six-piece band was playing for dancing the good old jazz of the Twenties and some pretty girls – pretty in the plump Russian style of Ostrovsky's plays – were out dancing with officers of the garrison and with civilians. The service was better and more cheerful than in Moscow. One sensed a desire to please rarely found in that over-extended capital and people seemed to be enjoying themselves in an almost Dickensian style. It is perhaps not so odd that Russians should until recently have envisaged England as Dickensian because provincial Russia still retains something of the atmosphere delineated by Phiz and Cruikshank. But we liked our first night out in a provincial town. Whether the Russians are wise to advertise Vladimir and Suzdal as major tourist attractions all over Europe as they are now beginning to do remains to be seen. If thousands of West Europeans and Americans descended on this simple place – would there be room for them? And would they, with one shower bath on each floor of a musty hotel, consider that ecclesiastical architecture alone was sufficient justification for their journey? I am no lover of ancient churches *per se* but we were to find that although Vladimir is really no more than a few churches preserved as the centrepiece of a new industrial town, Suzdal is something very different – something perhaps unique in Europe. Suzdal is a holy city (medieval in essence though with harmonious accretions of later date) which by a happy accident and thanks to the labours of one inspired archaeologist, Alexei Dmitrievich Varganov, has been preserved very much as it was in the days of Alexander Nevsky, who in the twelfth century became Prince of Vladimir by permission of the Tartar Khan whose seat was at Kazan on the Volga. (The Tartar Empire then extended all the way from Mongolia to the Caspian, with its capital at Samarkand.) In Suzdal the Soviet State is striving to do essentially the same job of restoration and reconstruction as the Rockefellers did at Williamsburg, the capital of colonial Virginia, but on a much larger scale and with inherently more splendid materials.

Suzdal lies some twenty miles from Vladimir in a belt of open country that looks like Salisbury Plain but is in fact the richest agricultural land outside the Ukraine. It was the wealth derived

Samarkand: the Gur Emir

from this granary which built the cathedrals and monasteries of Suzdal and as one drives along the Suzdal highway the power of the Orthodox Church can still be appreciated. Dotted across the horizon are large villages each dominated by the tall white tower and cupola of its church. Fifty years after their clergy left them these churches stand as strong as ever, like watch-towers over their villages, enabling the traveller to steer towards the place of his choice, over the open fields and paths, long before the low-lying wooden houses can be seen. No longer serving any Christian purpose, the church still marks the centre of each village. One can understand why the power of the church had to be broken before socialism could advance; the villages were never as poor as they look but architecturally they were – and are – ignoble while the church was rich and the only building of beauty in the community. And this remains true today.

The poet Vladimir Soloukhin, who was born in a village between Vladimir and Suzdal, has drawn attention to the contrast between the splendour with which 'the old ideology of Church and Tsar' took care to surround itself and the indifference shown by the Communist Party towards any kind of aesthetic embellishment in the countryside. In the cities there are Pioneers' Palaces, lavishly decorated underground railways and splendid opera houses that testify to the Party's boasted 'solicitude for people' but in the vast rural areas – nothing. As a countryman himself, Soloukhin is disturbed by this dichotomy. He has pointed out that the old world attached great importance to its ideology for these white-walled temples scattered all over the countryside were in fact strongholds of a régime. 'Their great bells filled the air with music more impressive than any Pathétique Symphony. Emerging from their dark noisome huts the peasants would suddenly find themselves in an environment of gold and perfume, with hundreds of candles flickering and melodious singing by the choir. It was enough to stir any heart, make any head whirl. In this way the old régime clothed its reactionary ideas in a film of beauty.'

And how, he asks, do we communists propagate our faith, splendid and magnificent as it is? As likely as not, you will see a few tattered wall posters in a squalid village club where nothing takes place except a weekly dance in which everyone wears overcoats and felt boots, a few games of chess or dominoes, an occasional film and a very dull lecture once a month.

Varganov has been working on the restoration of Suzdal for more than thirty years. When he first came he found a moribund village of some two thousand inhabitants with over forty churches and monasteries in a state of decrepitude. Some of the churches dated merely from the eighteenth century and the authorities at first proposed that only the architectural gems dating from the

Middle Ages should be preserved and all the rest pulled down. But Varganov managed to persuade them that the whole complex should be retained. The cost in time and money must have been prodigious and the task may not be finished in Varganov's lifetime. Many of the buildings are on an enormous scale. The Spasso–Yefimovsky Monastery, for example, is encircled by a rose-brick wall 3,600 feet long with watchtowers all around and a central gateway sixty feet high. The Pokrovsky Monastery, with its cathedral, is also an enormous construction and the Archbishop's Palace and the Rozhdestvensky Cathedral with its blue domes dotted with golden stars are even larger. Within Suzdal there are few paved roads, no railway station, no factories. The wooden houses which lie between the monasteries and often encroach upon them must have been built by a rich peasantry for they all have gardens or orchards. There are, for my taste, not enough trees and those that remain are too small and bent by winter gales but Suzdal is entirely uncontaminated by the industrial age. With geese honking on the greensward between the cottages and chickens running wild on the grassy streets and the cottagers burning wood, not coal, it is possible to imagine oneself back in the Middle Ages. Under the monastery walls the peasants are tilling small plots of land as they did then, women are washing their clothes in the streams and industrial Russia with all its gritty squalor seems as far away as industrial England. At present a certain squalor attaches to Suzdal too but I suspect it is that authentic medieval squalor which gave such verisimilitude to the films of Sergei Eisenstein. And indeed the Pokrovsky Monastery with its white walls and towers, set in green meadows, looks exactly like a set from *Alexander Nevsky*.

There used to be a small hotel which is now closed for modernization and there exists a somewhat ominous plan to build a 'tourist complex' on the banks of the River Kamenka and to turn the Pokrovsky Convent into an hotel and utilize the adjoining cathedral as a concert hall. At the same time all electricity cables are being put underground and asphalt roads are being taken up and replaced by cobblestones. An attractive colonnade of small shops first erected to commemorate the victory over Napoleon is being restored.

Tourists who may sleep in the Pokrovsky Convent in future should not be susceptible to superstitious fears for the place has a melancholy history. Founded in 1364 and rebuilt in the sixteenth century, it was used by the tsars and by noble families as a place where errant wives and daughters could be immured. The father of Ivan the Terrible, Tsar Vassili, found himself in the same situation as Henry VIII of England when the church refused to permit him to divorce his

Suzdal: medieval wooden church

barren wife, Solomonia, so that he might marry the Polish noblewoman Helena Glinskaya, who he hoped would give him an heir. For eight years the Tsar lavished gifts on the church and especially upon the Pokrovsky Convent, where he planned to send his wife as a nun, and finally the Metropolitan of Moscow sanctioned the divorce. Solomonia was removed with considerable brutality to Suzdal and the Tsar married Helena, who gave birth to the future Ivan the Terrible. But before this event Solomonia found herself pregnant and gave birth in the convent to a male child who was marked for death lest he might grow up to challenge Ivan for the throne. Before the Tsar could have the child killed, however, the boy was reported to have died a natural death and to have been buried in the convent. In 1934 Varganov opened the vault where the child was reputed to lie and inside a small wooden coffin he found the figure of a doll adorned with a silk shirt sewn with pearls. Varganov has no doubt that the burial was a fake, carried out to save the life of Solomonia's child, and he also believes that the child grew up to become the outlaw Kudeyar, a sort of Russian Robin Hood who roamed the forests with a band of followers throughout the reign of his reputed brother Ivan, and is the hero of many songs and legends.

The high walls of the Spasso–Yefimovsky Monastery also enclose dark secrets. Catherine the Great turned part of the monastery into a prison for political offenders. Anticipating a recent dark page in Soviet history, they were declared to be 'madmen' who needed the peace of monastic seclusion to recover their wits. But once inside the monastery they were never seen again. At the far end of the monastery courtyard there is a narrow gate which leads into a small close invisible from the outside. Opening off this are cell-like chambers whose windows are blocked by the high outer wall of the monastery. Beyond this again lie a number of secret cells reserved for high security prisoners. One of the Decembrists, Shakhovsky, was kept imprisoned here and finally lost his reason. These prisoners did not know in what part of Russia they were detained nor did the warders know the prisoners by name, only by a number. The prison was in use right up to modern times for Leo Tolstoy was once informed by a confidant of the Tsar that a cell had been prepared for him there in case he should carry out his unorthodox ideas beyond the limits of imperial tolerance.

Paul and I spent two days in Suzdal, driving over from Vladimir and stopping on the way at Bogolyubovo where stands the church of Pokrov on the Nerl, built by the Grand Prince of Vladimir in 1165 as a memorial to his son killed in battle. This little masterpiece in gleaming white stone stands in the water meadows not far from the prince's palace. The electrified main railway to Gorki runs close by and electric pylons straddle the fields behind it – an outrage which could easily be remedied – but the tiny church, in a country that boasts so much grandiloquent architecture, stands out like an exquisite Fabergé miniature in a collection of crown jewels. It was built by Vladimir craftsmen without any foreign assistance or inspiration and I think Russian architects are right to claim that it ranks with the Taj Mahal and the Petit Trianon at Versailles as one of the glories of our world. In winter the church can be reached on foot through deep snow but in the spring the flood waters leave it isolated on its island for weeks at a time. Paul and I approached it dry-shod on a day of howling wind which made one marvel that so delicate a structure could have withstood the savage elements of all the Russias for eight hundred years.

It is hard to imagine what the future of Suzdal will be. A party of elderly schoolmistresses from Moscow and ourselves were its only visitors in those two days. It is so much more remote from the modern world than any such place could be in Western Europe that it can be confidently recommended to anyone in danger of a nervous breakdown. There is nothing whatever to do except go around its innumerable churches and look at the splendid ikons and embroideries in its museum: there are no sounds except the cawing of rooks and the crowing of cocks and the passage on the high road of an occasional car. Suzdal exemplifies religiosity gone mad. But can Varganov logically restore every church and thus make Suzdal the largest complex of religious architecture in Europe without putting anything back into the churches? For they are all completely empty. Not one is used for worship – a 'working church', as the Russians say. The place is a graveyard of Orthodoxy which relies for its appeal on architecture alone. One wonders whether a summer pageant or a little *son et lumière* in season might not help?

Bukhara

4 SAMARKAND AND BUKHARA

Two influences from childhood have spurred me in the direction of Samarkand. One was the production of James Elroy Flecker's *Hassan* at His Majesty's Theatre in the 'twenties with Henry Ainley and Leon Quartermaine in the leading parts and with 'the golden road to Samarkand' as a leitmotiv which no romantic schoolboy could resist. The other was the circumstance that as a boy at King's School, Canterbury, I happened to be taught in the same classroom in which Christopher Marlowe absorbed, at a distance of only two hundred years in time, the blood-curdling history which set him on the path to writing *Tamburlane*.

Once during the war, when permission to visit Soviet Asia was almost unobtainable, I was told that I might go to Samarkand and Bukhara, only to have my editor cable me from London: 'Who wants Bukhara when you'll soon have Berlin.'

The flight of nearly two thousand miles from Moscow to Samarkand marked the start of our major swing through Soviet Asia and back to Leningrad by way of Georgia and the Ukraine. We set out with a clip of food coupons labelled *Bisnestour*. The Russian attitude to flying has become pedestrian because long-distance flights are now cheaper than train journeys. But the Russian language helps: to pack your *chemadan* before flying off to Samarkand in your *samalyot* has a resonance more romantic than merely packing a suitcase and taking a plane.

The airport of Domodedevo from which one flies to the Far East is a long drive from Moscow. It is rather larger than Sheremeteyvo but has already outgrown its function and a second airfield, equally large, is being constructed nearby. It was dark when we arrived but in the glare of arc lights the airport was as busy as Heathrow at midday. A big jet was just taking off for Vladivostok, a distance of some five thousand miles, but the embarkation was entirely routine because it was just a domestic flight. Our plane was an Ilyushin 18, a big turbo-prop, and the passengers were a good cross-section of Soviet society. A few years before they would have travelled in different classes in the train and taken some three days for the journey to Samarkand but the air has proved an even greater leveller in Russia than with us. There were a lot of army and air force officers, including a general, and many Uzbek and Kazhak collective and state farmers, together with some pretty sharp characters from Tashkent who looked like Neapolitan spivs in fur caps. One very statuesque Uzbek hostess dealt firmly with these rough types. When one rustic character spilled a bottle of gherkins in the gangway she made him clear it up himself. We took off with our lights down so that the children aboard could get some sleep but at one in the morning the hostess switched them all on and announced that supper would be served. Hearing that little food was offered on internal flights we had taken the precaution of getting a meal in Moscow and found it difficult to face cold chicken, cheese and fruit washed down with tea. No liquor is served on internal flights but there was plenty to be had at the airport bar before leaving. I had ordered a brandy and was given 100 grammes. Paul on this occasion preferred milk, of which some six different varieties were on offer, and he pronounced his choice to be the best he had ever tasted – ice cold and containing a great deal of cream. However, the early morning meal passed an hour or so and then the lights were dimmed again and presently turned out, for we were flying to meet the sun and long before we approached Samarkand the sky reddened and burst into flames. The runway at Samarkand is long but looks as if it had been a military one until recently. As we were to find in other places, a new air terminal was being built, together with an hotel to house the passengers from Europe who will soon be flying from Europe into Soviet Asia and beyond via Moscow in little more time than it now takes to fly from London to New York.

Samarkand lies at a height of 2,000 feet. The snow-capped Pamir mountains surround it on three sides at a distance of some twenty-five miles. The city is well irrigated, with poplars, orchards and vegetable gardens stretching in every direction. As soon as we stepped onto the tarmac we smelt the clear air of an Asian spring. The city suffers extremes of heat and cold but the climate is dry and judging by the brick-red complexions and robust frames of its natives, healthy. The Russians have been here only a hundred years but they have developed their conquest in a manner never attempted by us in India because they intended to stay – not to look over their shoulders towards retirement in European Russia as our administrators used to look forward to senescence in Cheltenham or Tunbridge Wells. Their hold upon Bukhara is even more recent. The former Khan of Bukhara lived on in his capital after the revolution and finally withdrew to Afghanistan in 1922.

As we drove into the city I was at once reminded of Teheran and its tree-lined avenues, or even of some British cantonment in northern India, and one could appreciate why the great Asian conquerors must have found themselves just as much at home here as they did in Persia, Afghanistan, Turkmenia or northern India. The whole of central Asia is climatically akin and the stylized pictures in the art of all these countries of recumbent, wine-bibbing poets, of polo players and khans out hunting with their falcons truthfully portray the unchanging character of this roof and watershed of the world. Some of the older Uzbeks we met along the way looked precisely like these pictures in their blue caftans and broad turbans lying flat on the head. One magnificent old gentleman with a long white beard was wearing a velvet robe of royal purple and long pointed shoes. He wore a necklace of amber beads and carried a white staff in his hand. The proportion of Russians to Uzbeks in Samarkand is said to be 10 per cent to 70 per cent, the remainder of the population of a quarter of a million being made up of Greeks and other minorities. We had slept little on the plane and the sunlight pierced our drooping eyelids with a painful intensity. The Samarkand Hotel backs onto a park where almond trees were in blossom and whence the sound of outdoor billiards, played beneath the trees with wooden balls, summoned one imperiously to slumber but an *Intourist* girl named Tamara – voluble, red-haired and alarmingly regimental – called us no less imperiously to our duty.

'The car is ready,' she declared, 'and the intellectuals of our city wait to see you. But first we see the ancient monuments, then our monuments of Soviet times.'

So, with nodding heads and itching bodies, we drove off in the noonday heat to absorb our ration of culture. The famous buildings of Samarkand create a melancholy impression because those that remain, after centuries of earthquake and human pillage, are nearly all monuments to the dead and not so often the glorious as the infamous and bloodthirsty dead. Samarkand is first mentioned by Greek historians in the fourth century A.D. when it was known as Marakanda after being captured by Alexander the Great. In the sixth century it became part of the Turkish

Bukhara: Citadel of the Emirs

BUKHARA: The Citadel of the Emirs

Khanate and two centuries later it was conquered by the Arabs. Marco Polo, in his turn, described Samarkand as one of the great cities of the world. Lying at the very centre of Asia, at the crossroads of the caravan routes from China, India, Mongolia, Persia, Caucasia and thence through Turkey into the Mediterranean world, the wonder is that anything of the ancient city remains at all, for apart from the earthquakes which have shaken it through the centuries, it was destroyed time after time by one historic conqueror after another.

Alexander levelled it to the ground after a revolt against his rule. The Arabs laid it low and the Mongols under Ghenghis Khan did the same. From the late fourteenth into the fifteenth century it was the capital of Timur the Lame, under whom it became the most important city in Asia. It was from Samarkand that Tamburlane sallied forth to conquer all of central Asia, Afghanistan, Persia and northern India and when he returned from his conquest of Delhi in 1399 with a great treasure of elephants, gold, precious stones and slaves he determined to build as a thank-offering the greatest mosque in the world. This is the so-called mosque of Bibi Hanum, named after Tamburlane's favourite wife, who is said to have been a Chinese princess of great beauty. It stands not far from the Registan, the great square in the centre of the city which Lord Curzon declared to be the most beautiful in the world. Curzon visited Samarkand before he became Viceroy of India and was inspired by what he saw there to rebuild Delhi on the same grandiose scale.

The square is lined on three sides with *medressehs*, or theological colleges, in one of which Timur's grandson, Ulugh Begh, is believed to have taught. Ulugh was the greatest astronomer of his age. The ruins of his observatory, which stand on a hill on the outskirts of the city, testify to that. But he was also a sort of imperial Bertrand Russell whose passion for reform burst out of the confines of his age. At this time the highest aim of Muslim education was to learn the Koran by heart. But Ulugh Begh declared that since the sciences came from God, they should be taught as well as religion in the colleges. The Mullahs would have none of this. In their view science came not from God but from the Devil. Ulugh Begh was regarded as a corrupter of the young, his studies of astronomy and mathematics akin to witchcraft, and when he was away from Samarkand on a journey he was waylaid by a gang of hired thugs and beheaded. Thus died the grandson of the ruffianly Timur, a ruler far in advance of his time, an intellectual who hated wars of conquest and whose astronomical calculations, though made with primitive instruments, have been found by modern scientists to be remarkably accurate.

The Mosque of Bibi Hanum was five years in the building by craftsmen who worked on it in relays, day and night. Tamara, in the flat sing-song all guides unhappily acquire after telling the same spontaneous story thousands of times, recounted what she called a 'curious legend' concerning its construction. The young architect chosen by Tamburlane to build the mosque fell in love with Bibi Hanum during the Khan's continued absence in India, and began to slow down the work because he could not bear the thought of leaving the queen's presence. When she upbraided him for his tardiness he said he would increase the tempo if she would permit him to kiss her. She replied that he might kiss any other member of the harem except herself. Calling for forty brightly decorated eggs, she broke them together in a bowl, and declared: 'Taste these eggs and you will see that though each one looks different, they in fact taste just the same. That is how it is with women.'

The architect then called for two vessels, one containing water and the other the pale white wine of Samarkand. And he said: 'Observe that the contents of these two vessels are indistinguishable, yet they taste very different.'

Bibi Hanum then permitted him to kiss her but, said Tamara, 'so hot was his kiss that it inflicted a burning mark on the queen's cheek which would not disappear.' When Tamburlane returned from India the amorous couple were terrified of his wrath but the Khan was so delighted by the beauty of the mosque that he forgave his wife's indiscretion and did not put the architect to death. However, as a means of concealing his own shame, he ordered every woman of his court to veil her cheeks in future. 'And that,' said Tamara blandly, 'is the reason why Muslim women go veiled to this day.'

Bibi Hanum is buried in the Shah-i-Zinda, the avenue of royal tombs which stretches up a hillside, each tomb splendidly decorated with mosaics, most having blue domes in which storks build their nests unless shooed away by the attendants. Tamburlane himself is buried in the Gur Emir, the most splendid of all the monuments whose great azure dome reflects the sunlight from its innumerable mosaics across the dun roofs of the menial houses that surround it. The Arabic inscription on the tomb declares him to be a descendant of Genghis Khan. Nadir Shah, the Persian conqueror, removed the green jade from the sarcophagus and took it with him to Delhi but later repented of his vandalism and sent the jade back again.

The Soviet archaeologist Gerasimov, who has specialized in reconstructing the likenesses of historical figures by using their skulls as a basis for sculpture, was recently allowed, after he had applied this method to Ivan the Terrible and other tsars, to open Timur's tomb. Having seen several of Gerasimov's reconstructions I was not impressed because all of them seemed to be siblings with pronounced Tartar features, but about the authenticity of Ulugh's grave at least there can be no doubt for when it was opened it was found that his head and trunk had been buried separately.

The sound of Uzbek music from Tashkent Radio came from a nearby teahouse. It did not mar the tranquil atmosphere of Timur's tomb. But the juke-box which had been blazing at breakfast-time when we had had a cup of tea at the hotel before starting out was another matter. I don't say the hotel should have had Asian maidens playing sackbuts and dulcimers for our entertainment but these Polish juke-boxes are certainly an atrocity.

After we had seen the ancient city Tamara began carrying out her threat to show us the new. We protested that we had not come to Asia to see pre-fabricated apartments designed in Leningrad. So we compromised with the opera house. This is not in the Stalin style but is functional and new. But when does an opera become an operetta? When, I suspect, it is sung in Uzbek in Samarkand. *Cho Cho San*, as the Russians call *Madame Butterfly*, was being given there that night but we decided to stay away and spend the evening in our hotel – a wise decision, as it turned out, for the hotel restaurant proved to be the gayest place in Samarkand.

The days when Russians were discouraged from mixing with foreigners and placed at separate tables when they met in cafés are past. On the contrary, as we were to find in Samarkand and in all the other places we visited, the problem for foreigners now is to secure seats for meals in their own hotels, so great is the influx of Russians into these establishments. However, occasions still arise when the old taboo is invoked. Finding every table but one filled, we took our places next to a solitary German. He told us he was a journalist from Bavaria and was 'on holiday – not working'. He had been in Japan and in Siberia and was now seeing Soviet Asia on his way home. He was young but very fat and wore a nondescript shirt and trousers which gave the effect of a Party uniform. He admitted having spent three hours at table already and to drinking each night a couple of bottles of wine followed by at least four bottles of beer. He sat at table like a great frog, never speaking to anyone but looking at every table in turn through sagging eyes overloaded with gall. After the briefest exchanges with us, he lapsed again into silence. If he is not a spy, I thought, he certainly looks like one. Is he perhaps carrying off a double deception, like those minefields we used to plant in the Libyan Desert which purported to be fakes but, when the attack came, turned out to be real? To send into Russia a spy so overwhelmingly Ambler-like that all who see him say: 'So felonious a character cannot possibly be real' might be as good a way as any of getting information. But on the other hand what secrets are available in Samarkand? The numbers of the army units that have been moved up to the Chinese frontier, perhaps . . .

Ignoring the presence of the German, since he chose to ignore ours, we went on to have a satisfying dinner of clear soup with meat balls, shashlik, salad and delicious unleavened bread. We drank vodka and two bottles of Uzbek *rosé*. The bill came to £1 5s. each.

The German had now been four hours at table without, apparently, exhausting the possibilities of the place. A queue of would-be customers stood behind the door, among them an Uzbek countryman with a marvellous Taras Bulba face. He had enormous moustaches and a mahogany complexion and he wore baggy Turkish trousers. I got up and asked him if he would like the free seat at our table. He accepted with a vulpine smile but before he had even got his nose into the menu our Russian waitress came up and asked him to leave. Paul and I protested at this arbitrary decision; while we were arguing, the German pulled himself together and shambled out of the room and our Uzbek friend meekly followed him and took his old place at the head of the queue. This left the waitress free to speak her mind.

'I couldn't let him join you with the German at your table,' she said.

'Why not? The German seems a lone wolf who speaks to no one.'

'No, but he listens. He sits there for hours at a time, listening to every word that's said. I don't trust him – do you?'

With more justification, our waitress reacted with severity against a party of Uzbeks in embroidered skull-caps who were having a birthday celebration at a neighbouring table. There were ten of them and they were drinking vodka and wine in a manner of which the Prophet would certainly have disapproved. One of them vomited on the floor. Immediately our waitress was upon them. Pointing to the door she cried: 'Out, the lot of you!' Without a word the ten men got up and left. They knew they had collectively breached the basic code of Soviet society. They had been guilty of an act that is *Ne kulturny*.

Most of the diners were countryfolk but a young couple dancing to the juke box were of a different calibre. The sight of them made me wonder whether the old Russian practice of naked bathing – there exists a picture of the last Tsar and his entire male entourage swimming in the nude – does not spring naturally from the immemorial deficiencies of Russian clothing. This girl had a very pretty Russian face with dark hair parted in the middle. Her escort was a Christlike young man with a blond beard. Their parents were probably officers stationed in Samarkand as part of the big army which is quietly being built up near the Chinese frontier. They were a handsome and well-bred pair, notwithstanding their poor clothes. The girl wore a sack-like dress of black serge. The young man, when he rose to hold back her chair, was seen to be wearing a suit of such a shiny, shabby texture as would not be worn in England by the meanest graduate of Borstal. His jacket, as he bent forward, shot up like a bum-freezer; his trousers were as wide as those of Grock the clown.

After the second bottle of wine, I longed to strip off their clothes myself and reveal them in their true beauty.

★   ★   ★

On the public square near the Registan stands a teahouse much favoured by countryfolk up for the day. A bus stop lies conveniently at its portal. It is a pavilion built of glass some hundred feet long with a huge Bukhara carpet covering the windows at one end and a portrait of Lenin hanging over it. Six enormous divans draped in carpets are disposed around the walls: as many as six or more elderly turbaned gentlemen were reclining on these divans with trays of food and pots of tea before them. A television set and a radio were placed within their reach. The rest of the pavilion was occupied by zinc-topped tables such as one might find in a French café and around these people were playing dominoes and sipping green tea, Chinese-fashion. The food was all replenished from a kitchen in the open air so the whole place was free of encumbrance. Several of the drinkers were reading the local Russian newspaper but little Russian was used in conversation; it was all Uzbek or Tadjik. We approached two of the most decorative old gentlemen to ask if they would object to having their portraits done. They acceded in the most courtly manner and when the rest of the pavilion saw what was going on, one or two other figures in long caftans and turbans approached the divan we had chosen and entered into conversation with its occupants, thus getting themselves included in the art class.

This was a more agreeable experience than that which befell Paul at the Shah-i-Zinda where a horde of little Uzbek boys crowded around, fingering his pencils and making concentration impossible. The most vicious of these lads suddenly swooped on Paul's pencil case and ran away with it. Some of the others gave chase but Paul dared not leave the rest of his artist's materials lest they should be taken too. He shouted for the custodian of the shrine who shrugged his shoulders but ultimately summoned a militia man. He in turn obtained the name of the delinquent from one of the other boys and went off to interview his mother and the headmaster of his school, promising to recover the pencils and return them to our hotel. Paul recalled how Edward Lear, after being caught in similar circumstances while sketching in remote places, had perfected a technique of shinning up a tree to escape the attentions of savage dogs or importunate peasants.

'But,' I said, 'there are no trees in the Shah-i-Zinda and if you'd climbed one of those rickety domes you'd probably have caused a landslide.'

During the three days we spent in Samarkand the militia exerted themselves to trace the culprit. But the pencils were never returned. They were at least half-an-inch thick, of a type which does not seem to exist in Russia, and as our journey progressed we found they were an irresistible attraction to the small boys of all ages who used to gather round Paul as he worked. '*Bolshoi Karandash*!' ('Whopping great pencil!') these onlookers used to exclaim in covetous tones. It says much for the innate honesty of Soviet people as a whole that this pilfering in Samarkand was the only depredation we experienced in nearly seven thousand miles of travel.

The secretary of the Writers' Union in Moscow, Mrs. Oksana Krugerskaya, had asked the writers' union in each republic we were visiting to help us and in Samarkand the secretary of the local union put himself at our disposal with great courtesy. Dushan Faizi is thirty-nine, a poet and playwright who writes only in the Uzbek tongue, which resembles Turkish. The other regional language, Tadjik, is akin to Farsi, or Persian. In Moscow one hears stories of 'millionaire writers' who lead lives of glamour and I was interested to find out how the literary world revolved in so remote a place as Samarkand. Mr. Faizi told me he has fifteen members of the union under his care; they are at the same time members of the all-Uzbek Union, with headquarters at Tashkent, which comprises 230 members in all. Faizi is, as might be expected, a member of the Party though many members of the union are not. I asked if he had been elected. He replied that he had been 'chosen' but that if in eleven years of office he had not measured up to the job he would have been sacked. Of his fifteen members two write in Russian, two in Tartar and the rest in Uzbek. There are about thirty budding authors in the Samarkand region – some at the university, some working for the radio or the Uzbek news agency – who write in their spare

Suzdal: the Pokrovsky Monastery

time and may, once they have published a book or two, apply for membership of the union. What, I asked, are the advantages of membership? Not, it seems, as great as one might suppose. Most of the fifteen elect do other work besides writing but once they become members they are entitled – no matter what their main job is – to one day off each week in addition to Sunday and to one month's 'creative holiday' each year, during which they may go to so-called 'rest homes' run by the Soviet Writers' Union in such places as Leningrad, Sochi, or at a country house in the Moscow region. They have to pay their own fare but get all their keep for the month at the expense of their local union. Faizi said there are a few full-time authors in Tashkent who have published many books and live on their royalties alone but apart from the help already mentioned, there is no direct subsidy. 'We don't believe,' he said, 'in giving stipends to literary people who talk about letters but don't do any real work.'

And what, I asked, had he himself produced? Five plays, mainly comedies, four of which had been staged and the latest, entitled *A Bride Has Come*, coming on shortly at the Uzbek Drama Theatre in Samarkand. His plays have not been done far afield but at theatres in Tashkent, Bukhara, Samarkand, Firghana and at Tormez, a small town on the Afghan frontier. He has also published four slim volumes of verse, one of which was translated into Russian and issued in Moscow.

'Mostly,' he said, 'my verse is about love – lyrical, you know. I am also moved by the need for peace and the history of my own people. My first poem was autobiographical, about a young Uzbek boy who fought in the Red Army and ended the war in Berlin. My latest, "The Mother", is about a woman whose son was killed at the front twenty-five years ago. She is still waiting, though all her friends have long since given him up. She can't believe he will not come back.'

This seems to be a favourite theme of minor Soviet poets but I thought it would be impertinent in a failed poet like myself to offer any comment. Faizi has not been west of Berlin but he has visited Afghanistan, India and Ceylon, which are of course only a short jet flight from his home, and one of his poems has appeared in an Urdu translation.

Who, I asked, are the best Uzbek writers today? He named four of whom, I had to admit with shame, I had never heard. Aibeck he considers the best novelist (one of his works has been published in England), Abdullah Kahar a good novelist and short-story writer and Zufiyah, whose surname is Israelova, the best poetess. Yashen, the chairman of the Uzbek Writers' Union, is a prolific playwright, well known in Tashkent.

Then we got down to the consuming interest of writers everywhere – money. Faizi said a novel is usually brought out in this manner – first it is published in one of the literary magazines as a serial, to give both reader and publisher some idea of its worth. Then, if chosen for publication between covers, it will probably have a first printing of 15,000. This would yield the author 7,500 roubles, or about £3,000. Writers in big demand might get first printings of anything between 25,000 and 100,000.

I remarked that most writers in England would give their ears for terms like these. I recalled that an internationally popular writer like Charles Morgan had been delighted to get £3,000 for one of his most successful books before the war.

'Perhaps,' said Faizi, 'but don't forget we are a small people with a language little known. When J. B. Priestley was in Samarkand in 1965 he told me that the great advantage English writers have over all others, apart from writing in the language of Shakespeare, is that they can be read all over the world. Perhaps this compensates them for getting not much money.'

'Also,' I said, 'English authors can write about any mortal thing they like. We have a Society of Authors, too, but we don't have a political appointee at its head.'

Faizi smiled diplomatically and went on to ask if I knew any English writers, apart from James Elroy Flecker, who had written about Samarkand. I recalled that Marlowe had made *Tamburlane* an appalling monster yet had provided splendid verse for him to speak.

'We must look it up,' said Faizi, 'for you see we are bringing out an anthology of writings about Samarkand, from the ancients down to the present and including work by foreigners, as our contribution to the celebration of the two thousand five hundredth anniversary of the founding of the city. We are inviting the mayors of all the world's ancient cities to come here.'

'Only the ancient ones?'

'Well,' came the prompt reply, 'only such cities as Rome, Damascus and Athens can stand comparison with Samarkand.'

It seems that Tamburlane had the same idea. For when he was building settlements in the countryside around his capital he named them after famous cities he had read about. So to this day villages nearby are called Baghdad, Paris and so on.

*   *   *

It takes only forty minutes to fly from Samarkand to Bukhara – just time for a charming little Uzbek air hostess to hand round sweets and glasses of sparkling Narzan water. The aircraft was an Antonov 18, the best-looking aircraft I had yet seen, powered by two very large turbo-prop engines. Its landing speed, however, seemed alarmingly fast for so small a plane. One flies over a wide, well-watered valley dotted with farms and villages. A rich-looking region, by Asian standards, and quite thickly populated, with only small patches of desert to be seen. Irrigation canals stretch in all directions.

Arab influence seems much stronger in Bukhara than it does in Samarkand. The mud brick is everywhere, the glazed tile rarely seen. Until the Arab invasion of the eighth century Bukhara was ruled by the Western Turks. It prospered under Arab rule and was ranked as a sacred city along with Damascus, Baghdad, Mecca and Medina. In the sixteenth century it boasted 400 mosques and the walls of the city were eight miles in circumference. Today its population is 100,000, of whom 10,000 are Russians from the R.S.F.S.R. and 10,000 indigenous Jews. The Bukhara *oblast* is twice the size of Holland and Belgium. Despite its lush appearance from the air, only 10 per cent is irrigated but it produces cotton, natural silk, and caracul fur, wine, gold and natural gas in great quantities. Bukhara carpets, it seems, were never woven in the town but were so called only because Bukhara was the market where all the rugs of Central Asia were sold.

The old city walls have been pulled down where they have not fallen down and except in one sector they are not being preserved because the art of making high walls of mud brick seems to have been lost. Around the tomb of Ismail Samani, the founder of the Samanid dynasty, however, a park is being laid out and one of the old city gates and a section of the wall is being repaired. The Samanid tomb dates from A.D.907 and since its occupant was regarded as a saint, generations of the faithful arranged to be buried close to him with the result that until 1934, when Soviet archaeologists started to clear the site, the tomb was almost smothered by the weight of graves around it. Now it has been opened up and its modest but ingenious brickwork must appear, in the dry desert air, almost as it did a thousand years ago. As Paul and I inspected the tomb we were approached by a television documentary team from Tashkent who asked if they might use us as 'extras'. They had no sound equipment with them and so they urged us to talk as much as we could in order to lend liveliness to the scene which, they explained, would be overlaid with romantic music in any case. So Paul and I walked around the site talking and gesticulating like Keystone cops.

'All these TV boys look alike,' Paul commented. 'This bunch, in their sweaters and corduroy jeans, could easily have come from Television Centre instead of Tashkent.'

'You don't think we're overdoing it?' I enquired. 'You *look* like an artist, so vivacity is expected of you. But I don't normally wave my arms about like this.'

'You're doing fine,' said Paul. 'You usually look like a Scandinavian diplomat. Now you look like one with St. Vitus's dance.'

Close to the tomb is Job's well, where Tamburlane is said to have eased his crippled leg. The prophet Job was evidently a water-diviner for when, legend says, he passed this way at a time of drought and struck a rock with his rod, a stream of medicinal water gushed forth. We sent a bucket down into the well and tasted the water. It is faintly saline but quite palatable. An Arabic inscription on the wall lists all the diseases which have been cured by the water – 'everything except diarrhoea and the common cold,' said the custodian proudly.

We went on to Registan Square, the centre of the ancient city, which is dominated by the Ark, a fortress dating from the first century, which was the winter residence of the Emirs of Bukhara. Opposite it is a mosque built in 1712 on the model of one in Isfahan. Its columns are made of cypress brought from India on elephants. The Ark has a more sinister ambiance than any building I was ever in. The Fortress of Peter and Paul at Leningrad or the Château d'If are pleasure domes by comparison. Part of this ambiance is theatrical, as we were to discover, yet the reality behind the peepshow must have been overpowering. The Emirs of Bukhara are not of ancient race and the image which they project is one of degenerate Muslim stupidity. After Nadir Shah of Persia conquered Bukhara in 1740 he set up a local ruler as his vassal and thirteen years later the Emir Mohammed Rahim freed himself from Persian rule and formed the Emirate, which endured until 1920.

The Ark is sixty feet high and covers an area of six acres. It is planned like a toy fort: a steep ramp just wide enough to admit four horsemen abreast winds up to roof level from the gateway but instead of a roof one comes to an open plateau. Here a great courtyard open to the sky is bounded on three sides by a pillared cloister. At one end the Emir's throne stands on a stone dais: the dais is shaded but the courtyard, with carpets spread over its paving stones, lies open to the sun so that all who approached the throne must have suffered discomfort. Opening out of the entrance ramp are a series of storehouses and dungeons. Here, in Soviet times, a sort of Madame Tussaud's exhibition has been mounted with the obvious intention of establishing the barbarity of the former Emirate. In the dungeons wax figures are seen hanging from the beams, their tongues protruding, while other unfortunates are shown in chains or scrambling for scraps of food thrown to them by warders. Higher up there is a museum in which are displayed some of the caftans, embroidered with gold and precious stones, which were worn at the Emir's court, together with pictures of prisoners having their throats cut by the Emir's guards. The walls are hung with instruments of torture including a vast bull-pizzle whip which used to hang over the Emir's throne – when it was not in use – as an emblem of sovereignty.

All this, if you like, is no more than a Chamber of Horrors installed many years ago by the Soviet authorities as a reminder to any nationalistic Uzbeks who might be tempted into nostalgia about the old régime. Yet the established facts about what happened to foreigners who entered the Emir's dominions are quite enough to underline the basic horrors of the régime. One Giovanni Orlandi, an Italian from Parma, was crushed to death because he could not make the Emir's watch keep good time. And in 1842, Colonel Charles Stoddart and Captain Arthur Conolly, sent by Queen Victoria to establish relations with the Emirate, were imprisoned for many months and eventually murdered on the Emir's orders. Not far from the Ark is the Pit, or smaller prison, where they were detained. It lies in an old quarter of mud houses quaintly roofed with straw in the hope of inducing storks, which are considered to be lucky, to nest there. And above the straw one sees TV aerials designed to trap the magic pictures from Tashkent. Around these houses hordes of little boys were playing. They crowded around us but unlike their contemporaries in Egypt or India they did not demand *baksheesh* nor were they crawling with flies.

At the bottom of the Pit, some forty feet below the ground and in almost complete darkness, wax models of the unfortunate English envoys can be seen, their clothes in rags and with snakes and scorpions writhing about the floor to torment them. This 'diorama' is quite accurate, in accordance with the report that was given in London at the time. But as to the official Foreign Office story that Stoddart and Conolly were put to death because they refused to embrace Islam one feels certain reservations. The Emirate of Bukhara was at this time a buffer state between British India and the Russian Empire but it lay much more in the Russian than the British sphere of influence. The Tsar's Government had sent missions to the Emir on several earlier occasions without mishap. In 1868 Bukhara became a vassal state of the Tsar and for some years before the Emir had received subventions from St. Petersburg. The arrival of the first British mission must therefore have been regarded with great alarm in Russia – and not only on political grounds.

BUKHARA stork

Although Bukhara was, by any standards, a slovenly and backward state, the Emirs were enormously rich thanks to the exploitation of a gold mine which they worked with prison labour so that its location should remain secret. Men who retired from working in the mine had their eyes put out so that they should not be able to reveal its secrets and anyone suspected of learning its location was immediately put to death. Quite apart from the political influence which the Russians exercised at the Emir's court, there could have been an even more potent argument for bringing about the destruction of the Englishmen. Had the Emir been given reason to suppose that the English envoys had found out – through bribery or other means – the location of his secret mine, he would never have let them leave alive.

For this mine was a very secret mine indeed. It was not located by the Soviet authorities until 120 years after Stoddart and Conolly were executed. Only in 1965 was the mine put back into production and it is now one of the richest in the Soviet Union. Indeed, a boom town has grown up around it.

Stoddart and Conolly received the honour of decapitation. Ordinary prisoners of the Emirs used to be cast down from the Tower of Death, a minaret 150 feet high which also had its uses as a place to call the faithful to prayer and as a sort of lighthouse; a fire used to be lit at the summit so that caravans approaching across the desert could locate Bukhara from afar. At its base there are a number of caravanserais, one for Indian merchants, one for Persians. Our guide here, determined to be 'with it', observed: 'One might say, a camel motel, yes?'

In the centre of the city there remain a number of 'active' mosques, notably the Mir Arab *medresseh* where fifty-two Islamic students spend a total of nine years, learning the Koran in both Arabic and Persian. We could see these young men walking up and down the cloister outside their cells intoning verses from the Koran which they held in their hands.

*   *   *

You can eat and drink well in Bukhara, even if the choice is never as large as the imposing menu suggests. On our first evening we had pickled mushrooms and salad, minced steak with peas, onions and sauté potatoes followed by the creamy yoghurt called Kefir. With this we drank a small carafe of vodka (100 grammes), two bottles of the local white wine and a glass of port apiece. We finished off with some Bulgarian cigarettes, which I found better than the local Russian ones.

The bill for this came to just over £1 per head at the official rouble rate, which certainly does not favour the English. It is a very long time since I can remember getting such a meal in London at such a price. In the environs of Bukhara they produce some excellent wine. The two best white wines are called Bishty and Bayanshirey. The best red is Kizil Mousalas.

The Bukhara and Samarkand hotels are identical, but the one in Bukhara has the gayer atmosphere and the service is quicker. In order to encourage local people to patronize the restaurant, they close the entrance from the hotel so that residents have to go out into the street and enter through a side door, adjoining which there is a summer café. The result is that the restaurant does a roaring trade, serving meals from morning till night except between the hours of two and four when the staff take a rest. It is hard to believe that these hotels came into being only in 1958 when the area was first opened up to foreign tourists. Their decorations and plumbing have taken a bad beating: is this because most tourists stay only a couple of days and move on, taking some of the plumbing with them? When Paul attempted to take a shower, the hot tap crumbled to pieces in his hand. Sallying out into the passage in search of someone to turn off the stream of boiling water he met an American woman on the same mission carrying a severed faucet in her hand. They had not exchanged many condolences before they established a common acquaintance among the dons of a small college in New England.

The American lady was overjoyed to hear an English voice. She did not speak a word of any other language save German and being ignorant of the Cyrillic alphabet she could not read a menu or a street name; nevertheless her husband had sent her on an elaborate holiday through Russia, travelling everywhere by air. It must have cost him six or seven hundred pounds. From each new town she sent him a cable and received from him an encouraging reply. You could not call her a Gertrude Bell or a Freya Stark of the jet age because she made no contact with the natives apart from the *Intourist* guides who ordered her meals and drove her to the ancient sites which she captured in colour with her ciné camera. She appeared to be lonely and not a little frightened. In retrospect, no doubt, her holiday would seem a glorious adventure. But not yet.

'Gee, it's oppressive, don't you find?' she said to Paul. 'How *can* they do the things they claim to do in space when they can't seem to do the simplest things on the ground?'

This proved to be the prevailing reaction among American tourists we met with the exception of a group of Jewish ladies from the Bronx, who perhaps because their assimilation was incomplete, seemed to be infused with old-fashioned Russian patriotism which made them enthusiastic about everything they saw in their former homeland. They bought Uzbek skull-caps and peasant embroidery at every opportunity and, wrapping themselves in shawls, soon succeeded in making themselves look much more Russian than American. But this lonely lady was almost as brain-washed as a Russian Party hack. To her every aspect of Russia was atheistically sinister.

'Before you arrived,' she said, 'I was the only European in Bukhara. If I'd been dying in the hotel last night I couldn't have summoned help because not a single soul could speak a word of English.'

A courageous woman, one had to admit. I couldn't imagine my wife nor the wives of any of my friends travelling all over Russia alone but neither could I imagine them attempting such a thing without a little linguistic preparation. The American lady joined our table for meals and sat close to us when we flew on to Tashkent.

When Paul complained to the manager about the plumbing he said it wasn't worth repairing because both the Samarkand and Bukhara hotels were 'worn out' and would be replaced, next year, by new ones. Smugly, perhaps, I felt bound to defend these Uzbek hotels. They were a great deal better than provincial hotels I had stayed in in Persia and Iraq. After all, we were in Central Asia, not on the French Riviera. And here, as in every other hotel we sampled, one could plug one's electric razor into the prescribed socket with confidence. This carried little weight with Paul, who could leave his beard untrimmed until we got back to Moscow, nor, perhaps, with the romantic heart of Brigadier Sir Fitzroy Maclean, M.P., who set out ahead of us to travel by train for seven hours across the desert to Khiva, which was just being opened up to foreigners. But in a hot climate I find it agreeable to have smooth cheeks.

Not so the cloakroom attendant in the hotel, whose resemblance to the late Joseph Stalin was so striking that one felt it must be cultivated. A Tadjik who spoke little Russian, he wore a heavy Stalin moustache, an old Party uniform into which one arm was thrust as though it were withered, and a cloth cap. I attempted to tell him that he reminded me of a famous personality and he seemed to understand for he struck a forbidding pose and assumed a terrifying scowl. Of course, he had the image quite wrong. When one saw Stalin in the flesh he did not look at all tough or aggressive. He had strong but delicate features, he was well made and graceful in his movements. His expression was shrewd but relaxed, the voice quiet; if little escaped the dark eyes, their gaze was more often amused than sardonic.

Stalin could, when he needed to, charm a bird off a tree. Our ambassador, Archibald

Clark-Kerr, said to me once when Churchill was in Moscow: 'The old man has fallen under Stalin's spell. There's no other word for it – he is eating out of Joe's hand.'

It struck me as odd that this Tadjik seemed to have modelled his impersonation of Stalin upon the crude stock figure one used to see in Western cartoons. Where could he have seen such an image? I asked him where he had been in the war: he proudly replied: 'All the way to Berlin.' Had he come across a *Völkischer Beobachter*, even a *Daily Mail*?

★   ★   ★

It had rained heavily in the night and was still raining at breakfast. The mud brick houses of the old city assumed a stained, grey texture as though they belonged to some industrial slum in Flanders instead of to Asia and when I set out to visit Alayev Said, who is reader in Uzbek literature at the teachers' college, I found the usually dusty side roads deep in mud. Mr. Said lives in his own house up an unmade road some distance from the centre of the city. There is a small garden at the back in which he grows hyacinths, roses and vegetables in deep trenches which have to be irrigated, although today they were awash. Cheerful farmyard noises came from the nearby houses but Mr. Said, unlike his neighbours, keeps neither chickens nor sheep. A large iron bedstead lay on the back porch, doubtless for summer siestas. On entering the house I took off my muddy shoes and put on slippers. The house appeared no larger than an English bungalow but the ceilings were high and my host had a fine study extending the full width of the building with glass-covered book-cases running around the walls, a desk at one end and a dining table and chairs at the other. Evidently the room was used as a dining-room on special occasions as well as a study. Before long I was to appreciate just how special this occasion was.

My host, wearing an embroidered skull-cap which gave him a somewhat patriarchal air although he was in fact only forty-seven, gave me a seat at the table, which was set for tea, and explained that while waiting for two friends he had invited to join us we would take some light refreshment. It was just after ten o'clock and I had had a large breakfast. I knew that some display of appetite was expected of me but I sought to put off the gastronomic ordeal for as long as possible by taking an interest in Mr. Said's library. He showed me a Shakespeare published in Tashkent in Uzbek, and volumes of Byron, Burns and Bernard Shaw in both Uzbek and Russian. He explained that students of Uzbek have had a difficult time since the revolution because up to 1929 the language was rendered in Arabic characters; from then until 1940 the Latin alphabet was used and since then it has been written in Cyrillic. This final rationalization has cheapened the cost of printing, typewriting and telecommunications but the process has not facilitated the writing of Uzbek literature. He praised the talents of Faizi in Samarkand – and not only in literature.

'Before his first child was born, our friend Faizi wrote a poem saying that despite the old Uzbek idea that only boys count, he would welcome a daughter. This progressive wish was granted. And it was granted again. And again and again until Faizi had nine girls. I pass no judgment on the literary merit of that particular poem but, you know, he ought not to have written it.'

Mr. Said himself had not been backward in that department, however. He told me he had seven children and his first grandchild had arrived only the week before. His wife he described as a wonderful woman for despite this intense family life she had protected his privacy so that he was now writing a thesis for his doctorate on the art of comedy, with special reference to Shakespeare's comedies, and yet she had found time to teach in a junior school herself. He told me that of Shakespeare's tragedies he preferred *Othello*. I said that when my wife, who had been trained as a Shakespearian actress, had to dub the part of Desdemona for the Russian film of that name she faced a problem for which the Old Vic had not prepared her. The Russian Desdemona spoke her Russianized Shakespeare with lip movements which simply did not accord with the English verse. Some Russian close-ups could not be cut because they were vital to the action so the only solution was to find English lines which would fit the Russian lip movements.

We went on to talk about the remarkable colony of Bukhara Jews, numbering some ten thousand, who came here from Shiraz and from Baghdad before the Arab conquest and have maintained their synagogues and their culture in Bukhara down to the present day. They have never spoken Hebrew, though their rabbi preaches in that tongue, but have retained Persian as their first language. It is likely that among these Jews there are distant relatives of the English Sassoons whose addiction to fox hunting and racing cannot have been acquired in the bazaars of Baghdad though their skill in banking seems to have been a shared inheritance. The Bukhara Sassoons were bankers to the Emir and their community as a whole was not persecuted in Central Asia as it was in Europe. Today the Bukhara Jews are active as musicians, artists and writers all over Uzbekistan. Alayev Said named as leaders of the community two colleagues of his at the college, Jacob Davidovich Pinhasov, a poet, and Yuri Israelovich Pakanaev, a reader in chemistry. And he showed me a history of Uzbek literature from the earliest times down to the seventeenth century written by Nathan Mouradevich Malayev.

Two other guests then arrived – Toshpulat Hamid and Mourad Halil, both poets and literary journalists. They were sturdy middle-aged men with battle-scarred faces – no doubt because the older generation of Uzbeks has gone through a very tough time. Mrs. Said, assisted by one of her daughters, then brought in plates filled with nuts, raisins, halva, pomegranates, pears, potato chips in exotic shapes and a variety of breads, some unleavened and some partly risen with a delicious glazed crust. With this we were to drink green tea taken with sweetmeats. Our host rose to his feet and ceremonially broke the bread, arranging it in large fragments before each guest. The quantity before me was such as I could hardly have got through in a week. Scarcely had we made a slight impression on this groaning board than Mrs. Said retired to the kitchen, returning with a huge plate of the national dish, Mantee – spiced minced meat in a case of pastry, topped off with sour cream and eaten with rice. This was accompanied by vodka and champagne.

When I weakly observed that this looked like a wedding feast, my host politely cut me short.

'Don't you believe it,' he said. 'At a wedding we would have five or six hundred guests and the feasting would last more than a day.'

It was still only mid-morning, the rain had ceased and in the stark sunlight my eyes began to feel as glazed as the pastry, but fortunately these Uzbeks had amplified the Russian custom of toasting by delivering a lengthy speech or reminiscence each time the glasses were raised and this enabled one to spend quite a lot of time on one's feet, mercifully immune from the proffered dish, the heaped spoonful.

Alayev raised his glass with a quotation from Omar Khayyam, first in Persian, then in Uzbek, about the joys of drinking. 'One should drink either with clever fellows or with a woman.' Hamid produced yesterday's Bukhara newspaper and read from it his latest poem about a boy who lived on the fourth floor of a city apartment but who tired of this luxury because he longed to go home where he could be woken at cock-crow, hear the sheep bleating and smell the green fields. Halil recited a poem of his about the beauties of natural gas. It had an insistent rhythmic beat which was meant to represent the roaring of a well that has gone 'wild'. The occasion celebrated had occurred three years before when gas had been struck fifty miles from Bukhara and could not be put out, so that the city was lit up at night by the glare until aircraft were called in to bomb the gusher and, by causing earth to block the hole, finally put it out.

When he sat down he filled in the unpoetic details. 'There's enough gas there to last two hundred and fifty years, we can use as much as we like for only nineteen kopecks a head for a month and we're building a pipe-line two thousand miles long to supply Moscow.'

Having no verse of my own to recite and being unable to remember anyone else's – save only the most scabrous limericks – I fell back on reminiscence. My theme would have bored an audience to tears in Cheltenham or Tunbridge Wells but here in Bukhara it was received, to my delight though not altogether to my surprise, with avidity. I told them I was the first member of my family ever to form a connection with Russia. For the previous 150 years my forefathers had been operating on the other side of the Pamirs – sometimes only a few hundred miles from where we were seated – on the northern frontiers of India. Long before the Russians came to Bukhara, my people had been in Baluchistan, in Sind and the Frontier Province. They were, of course, imperialists but imperialists of a more sophisticated kind than those categorized by Karl Marx. The Queen-Empress they served and the Russian Tsar were rivals for the affections of Central Asia and in the long run, of course, Russia had won: the English were separated by thousands of miles from their parent civilization whereas the Russians were based firmly on their own frontier. But, I said, the civilization which the Victorian captains represented in India was far more advanced than the Russian society of that time. For instance, the younger brother of my great-grandfather, General John Jacob, was a lifelong admirer of Republican England. He declared that he modelled Jacob's Horse and the other regiments which he founded on the principles of Cromwell's New Model Army. In 1858, before the liberation of the serfs in Russia, he wrote that although the British should occupy Quetta because it was the key to the Bolan Pass through which any invader must enter India, they should not thrust any deeper into Asia because, in the long term, they had nothing to fear from Russian competition. British sovereignty, he said, was maintained in India by a mere handful of English gentlemen; if they behaved as gentlemen should, no one could wrest India from them; if this standard was abandoned, they would deservedly lose their dominion. And I quoted General John thus: 'If Russia brings with her advance a better civilization and a higher moral tone: if she introduces European honesty, ideas and European commerce into Central Asia – the better for us. All that tends to good must ultimately be to the advantage of free England. But can Russia do this? Can she make known to the clever Asiatics a better, nobler and higher moral power than they are now acquainted with? I much doubt it.'

'Your ancestor was quite right,' said Alayev Said. 'Of course Tsarist Russia could do no such thing. For years she allowed the Emirs of Bukhara to rule with the utmost barbarity. Am I right in saying you would not have allowed an Indian Prince to do what he did?'

'We would not. But, to be fair, we were the sovereign power whereas Bukhara in those days was only a dependency.'

'Only when Soviet power came here,' said Halil, 'was it possible to change our old world. Only then did the Emir pack up and migrate to Kabul; he lives there still and they say his jewels still come onto the Kabul market from time to time. But one of his sons chose to remain. He is now a schoolmaster in Moscow.'

'And on *my* side of the frontier,' I said, 'the English have all gone home. The "native gentlemen" whom John Jacob insisted must be treated as the equals of his English officers now command the regiments which he raised: the city of Jacobabad which he founded still bears his name and his tomb and statue there are maintained by the Pakistan authorities. But otherwise, the old dreams of the English in India are over.'

'What, I wonder, would your ancestor think if he could be here in your shoes today?'

'It would sadden him, I think, to find Russian civilization installed in Central Asia while English civilization has withdrawn from India altogether but, in view of the kind of man he was, he would not be surprised. At least he was right in predicting that Tsardom was no match for English liberalism.'

And what, said my hosts together, would he make of Marxism–Leninism?

'I believe he would understand it. He was never a Christian and he believed that if the English must have a state religion, they ought not to parade it in India. In the fortress which he built in Jacobabad he amassed a library of thirty thousand volumes and from there he published pamphlets advocating a materialist philosophy founded on doctrines of evolution which anticipated Darwin. Had he lived until 1867 when *Das Kapital* was published, I think he'd have taken it in his stride.'

No sooner had I sat down than food and drink were again urged upon me in intimidating quantities. I must have flashed an S.O.S. to Mourad Halil for he rose to his feet again and, regarding the groaning board with an understandable emotion, raised his glass of champagne. 'The toast I would raise above all others,' said he, 'is not to literature, not even to our guest from England but to give thanks for the good health our people now enjoy. I put that above everything.

In my family there were eleven and nine of us died from various diseases. My father was a scrivener who copied the Koran for a living. In our house there were neither windows nor heating though at times here we have snow. Of sanitation there was none whatever and diseases multiplied through the contaminated water. We used to drink from the open *joub*. There was never enough to eat. And in the last days of the Emir, Bukhara had just two doctors and four beds for all the sick of the region. We weren't just backward then, let's face it – we lived like animals. You know the Soviet Union from the past and are travelling now to parts of it I have never seen, and maybe you are disappointed in the way life has developed, here and there. But for us in Central Asia there can be no disappointment: to us something quite fundamental has happened. For the first time in all our history we are living like men.'

I felt the diffident touch of Alayev Said's arm on mine. 'I trust you don't think that was propaganda?' he enquired.

'Not even *propaganda fidei*. I am sure it is true.'

Tiflis: the Kura

5 BIG CAP COUNTRY

The *Intourist* booklet on Georgia opens delightfully: '*There is a legend that 1,500 years ago King Vakhtang Gorgasali went hunting in the woods near Mtskheta, the ancient capital. His falcon was chasing a pheasant when it suddenly dropped into a pool and got boiled.*' Hence the origin of the city of Tbilisi, or Tiflis, for the hot springs thus discovered caused the king to shift his capital thither. 'Tbili' is the Georgian word for 'hot'.

I had been in Azerbaijan during the war on a visit to units of the Red Army which were being trained there as a reserve in case the Germans should break into the Caucasus but I had never been in Caucasia proper. All I knew about Georgia was that it was ruled for over a thousand years by Christian monarchs who had nothing in common with Russia and that the sturdy mountaineeers of Georgia prided themselves on inhabiting a European enclave in Asia which had preserved its national identity against all invaders until the Russians arrived as the protecting power some 170 years ago. My friend Professor David Lang, who is highly regarded in Georgia as the leading English expert on the country, has convincingly explained why a series of European statesmen from Palmerston down to Lloyd George and Poincaré failed in their efforts to use Georgian nationalism as a lever against Russia. In Tsarist times this was due to the identification of a large part of the Georgian nobility with the Empire despite the overbearing behaviour of many of the Russian Governors in Tiflis. In Soviet times, hopes that 'Christian feudal Georgia' might become a thorn in the side of the godless Soviet régime have foundered because the West was ignorant of the economic factors which made the Georgian people receptive to Marxism. In 1900, after one hundred years of Russian rule, the Russian imperial government actually owned some 58 per cent of the land in Georgia. The Georgian nobility owned 31 per cent and of the remaining 11 per cent a good deal belonged to individual members of the Romanov family. The peasants, forming over 80 per cent of the population, had only 6 per cent of the land and were also subject to heavy taxes and tithes. Georgia had been Russianized in the crudest possible manner so that when the young Stalin left the Tiflis theological seminary at the age of nineteen in 1898 – much to his devout mother's distress – he was quite truthfully able to equate all his people's misfortunes with the hated misrule of an alien imperialism. Nor was it only Russian landlords who were to blame. The ineptitude of the Russian ruling class had brought many foreigners into the Caucasus and many of the mines, oilfields and new factories were not run by Russians at all but by German, French and British entrepreneurs.

Georgia may or may not be the land of the Golden Fleece but nature has made it a veritable Cockaigne, a land not only of milk and honey but of vineyards, orchards, rich plantations of tea and tobacco, and underlying the magnificent scenery, both Alpine and sub-tropical on the Black Sea coast, lie rich deposits of coal, manganese and other minerals. Racially and culturally, the Georgians have nothing in common with the Slavs but so long as the Kremlin ensures that Georgia is not overrun by Slav 'settlers' and continues to be administered, as it is today, by native sons, one cannot see this small country wishing to forgo the advantages of being linked with the second largest industrial complex in the world.

Out of a population of $4\frac{1}{2}$ million, 65 per cent are now Georgian, 11 per cent Armenian, 10 per cent Russian and the rest Azerbaijanis, Ukrainians, Tartars and Kurds.

The lonely American lady flew with us as far as Tashkent. For some reason we swung some way east of the city before coming in to land and I calculated that at one point we were only 200 miles from the frontier of China. We teased the American lady about this. Indicating the inhospitable mountains to the east, we asked her to imagine the indignation of the State Department if by some mischance we were compelled to make a forced landing 'over there', and she, with her passport valid for everywhere except the Chinese People's Republic, North Vietnam and Cuba, set foot on this unAmerican soil. But she teased us in return. 'If you guys end up in the cooler I'll read about it back home. I've had enough. I'm pulling out and going home today.' She had cancelled the rest of her trip and was changing planes at Tashkent to fly to New York, via Kiev and Warsaw.

Kiev market

When we climbed into the big Ilyushin for Tiflis we were surrounded by Georgian faces, homeward bound. Across the aisle from us sat a Georgian version of Eliza Doolittle's father. His swarthy face quite blue with several days' growth of beard, he looked as if he had just hoisted a cartload of coal. With him were his three gypsy-like children. They had never been in a plane before and wanted to touch and to see everything. One of them was air-sick for most of the journey. The father coped with the emergency very well with the minimum of help from the air hostess, who was busy serving cold lunch and tea to the passengers. I developed a fellow-feeling for the Georgian coal-heaver, knowing only too well what it is like for a father to travel unaided with small children, and knowing, too, that I would not have acquitted myself so well.

At first we flew within sight of the snowy Pamirs and then rose higher to cross the great expanse of the Kara Kum Desert. We flew over the Caspian at its narrowest point and passed over Baku, in whose empty *Intourist* hotel I had once spent an unexpectedly convivial evening with Churchill's interpreter, Major Birse. Now it is a city of over a million inhabitants and its oil derricks stretch for miles into the sea. Soon a great snowy head and shoulders appeared far to the south – Mount Ararat – and then as we approached Tiflis the silvery peaks of the Caucasus pushed through the clouds, scarcely distinguishable from them until one saw here and there patches of dark brown rock that had lost their snow cover. We were not much higher than these peaks and one had the impression that the pilot was picking his way with care since all the approaches to Tiflis are ringed by mountains and even the runway itself is hillbound on every side.

We were met at the airport by a guide called Basil, a young man wearing a turtle-neck sweater, smoking American-type cigarettes and speaking a monosyllabic type of American English which he said he had acquired at the Tiflis school of foreign languages.

'You know James Aldridge?' he enquired. 'A swell guy. William Golding? Just dandy. Right now Stanley Kunitz is in town. A lovely person.'

He told us he didn't reckon on staying with *Intourist* for long, being ambitious to join the Soviet Diplomatic Service or maybe become an interpreter at the United Nations. Quite soon we formed the impression that Basil's ambitions were running a long way ahead of his abilities. His knowledge of the history and the amenities of his native city seemed extremely sketchy, or perhaps he had run through the standard *Intourist* patter so often that he couldn't be bothered to repeat any of it for our benefit. To many of our questions he returned an off-hand 'Search me' or 'You mebbe right'. Had he modelled himself on the English rather than the American moronocracy, he might have rewarded us with the classic: 'I couldn't care less.' The first and only time that we established any *rapport* with him was when we halted at the twelfth-century Zion Cathedral where lie the tombs of all the Georgian ruling princes up to the time of the October Revolution, where the Georgian Queen Tamara and the Russian Prince Yuri Bogolubsky who ruled in Suzdal were married 800 years ago, and where Stalin's mother is buried. A service was in progress and a score of elderly men and women were kneeling before the altar, bowing their heads and crossing themselves. The air was sultry with incense and gilded by the light of innumerable candles. When we came out Basil asked me if I believed in God.

'In the sense that he is referred to in there,' I replied, 'certainly not.'

'I am glad,' said Basil and he held up two linked fingers before my face as though, together, we had lost a whole worthless world.

When we got to the hotel, however, we decided to dispense with Basil's services and to explore the city alone. We went first to the old city, the Ortachala, which lies between the main thoroughfare, Rustaveli Boulevard, and Mount Mtatsminda, which towers 2,000 feet above it. The space between the Kura river and the mountain is narrow so that the tree-lined streets and squares incline steeply up the lower slopes until they end at the rock face. Many of the houses had once been the town residences of the Georgian nobility but had come down in the world and were now split up into flats and single rooms – but their overhanging balconies and shuttered windows still gave them an air of elegance and reserve. Some had iron gates through which carriages had once passed into a courtyard at the back, others had patios where orange trees stood in tubs and fountains still played. In one square, in the shadow of the castle which the Persian invaders built in the Middle Ages, stood a blue-painted house with a hanging gallery where the poet Lermontov had lived. It is now in the care of an old Russian lady who will show you the rooms he occupied – not for money but in exchange for cosmopolitan chatter. But the house is not a museum and the rooms are unremarkable. On the roadway that skirts the river bank we came to a synagogue. It was in full cry. The doors stood open: elaborate chandeliers blazed within and men in black homburg hats or in the huge aerodrome caps we had remarked in Moscow passed in and out. Paul observed that the aerodrome seemed to have become the national head-gear in Georgia and that we ought to call this chapter 'Big Cap Country'. Certainly every male who came within range of Paul's pencil seemed to be wearing one of these things and the shops were full of them at the equivalent of £3 apiece. Further on we came to a blue mosque built by

TBILISI: Lermontov's House, Alaverdova Square in the Kura district

Tiflis: house of the poet Lermontov

Azerbaijani Muslims. A crowd of slender black-eyed boys gathered around to tell us that the place was no longer a mosque but a *banya*. What did this mean? asked Paul. It could mean a bath-house, I replied, or perhaps a bordello. But when we observed the sequence of matronly women who were passing in and out of its doors its function could not seriously be in doubt.

On the other side of the Kura river we found men at work on a rocky promontory erecting a statue of the founder of the city, King Vakhtang Gorgasali. It is another Bronze Horseman but not, alas, as fine as the statue of Peter the Great in Leningrad. The King was already mounted on the front of his charger but the rear end of the horse lay on the ground with its legs in the air, like some property left over from a pantomime. By this time we had walked enough and hailed a taxi to take us back to the hotel but the driver, with a pepper-and-salt aerodrome pulled down over his swarthy features, was in no hurry to oblige us. Pointing to a men's lavatory across the road, he observed: 'That comes first' and disappeared inside. No other cabs were in sight so we stood by the parked vehicle waiting for the driver to reappear. The minutes lengthened into a quarter of an hour and still he did not come. Unless he had an escape route at the back it seemed that the driver must prefer this malodorous spot to our company. We decided that it was a long time since anyone had indicated so pointedly that he did not care for our faces and, abandoning our vigil at length, trudged back to the hotel on foot. It was evening now and crowds of promenaders were strolling under the trees along Rustaveli Boulevard. We looked in vain for dark-eyed Georgian beauties: most of the women were excessively hirsute, sallow-faced and short of leg. But the young men strolling together hand in hand were in the main handsome and merry-eyed. We had heard the Georgians were pleasure-loving, indifferent to money or status and ready to live for the hour, and our first impressions confirmed this. The older men had the air of Frenchmen from the Midi – rotund, well-liquored and evidently devoted to the pleasures of bed and board. We began to feel a strong attachment to this sunny, relaxed city. One might almost be in Sofia, said Paul, or perhaps Bucharest. But we decided that one cannot really compare Georgia with anywhere else: far from being just another Soviet republic it seems to be a unique country with a strong national identity.

The Hotel Tbilisi is like a good hotel in a provincial city of France. It stands on Rustaveli Boulevard, close to the old Governor's Palace, the opera house where Chabukhiani is still master of the ballet and the Georgian drama theatre. At one side it overlooks a church and the gardens of the art gallery and from the rear it offers a splendid view over the city, which sprawls

across the adjoining hills in every direction. I took to this hotel at once and would recommend it to anyone. I had an enormous room containing a three-piece suite, a dining-table and chairs, two beds and a bathroom of Roman proportions through whose wide windows one could watch the twinkling lights of the city as one lay in the bath at night.

The dining-room has a gallery running around it at first-floor level and marble pillars supporting a domed glass roof as in some transatlantic liner in the days when seagoing Kaiserins and serene highnesses required marine architects to match the grandeur of their surroundings on land. Farther along the boulevard a new 22-storey hotel is going up but if I go to Tiflis again I know which one I shall choose.

At dinner the first night we had a smoked river fish tasting very like salmon, followed by Chitshi-Pitshi, a Georgian mince dish somewhat like the Greek moussaka with a topping of creamed eggs, olives, onions and green peppers. The Georgian wine and brandy were excellent though at breakfast next morning we could not compete with the many robust Georgians who were taking a tot or two of brandy with a lemonade chaser before going on to fried eggs and Russian tea.

We were engaged that day to dine with Joseph Nonashvili, who had just been elected to the Supreme Soviet of Georgia and proposed to take us to visit his constituency, which lay over a hundred miles east of the capital in the midst of a wine-growing district. Travelling with us would be Stanley Kunitz, the American poet who has translated Pasternak and Vosnesensky and has won the Pulitzer Prize with his own verse. Kunitz was on an official lecture tour and so was accompanied by an attaché of the American Embassy in Moscow. Paul shrank from the idea of getting mixed up in anything like an official cultural beano. 'It'll be another Potemkin trip,' he said. 'Smiling peasantry on display and far too much to drink.'

'Surely,' I said, 'we have enough experience to discount surface manifestations and extract what we can from the trip. Besides, as Basil said, Kunitz is "a lovely person".'

Kunitz proved to be indeed a most interesting character. 'Filling us in' on him in advance, the very white-Anglo-Saxon-protestant young man from the embassy said: 'Stanley's career is as romantic as any Russian's.' The son of Jewish parents, the father from Prussia, the mother from Latvia, Stanley had 'come up the hard way'. His mother had come to New York from Latvia when only thirteen, without any money or assistance. She took a job as a seamstress before marrying Kunitz *père* and for a while they ran a prosperous cloak-and-suit business until their partner absconded, leaving fifty thousand dollars' worth of debts. The father committed suicide but the mother went on working, determined to repay all the creditors; at the same time she scraped and saved to send her son to Harvard where he eventually graduated *summa cum laude*.

His tour of Russia was going very well. At the universities of Kiev and Tiflis upwards of 400 English students had come to hear him reading his translations and his own works, and had given him a standing ovation.

Joseph Nonashvili liked to think of himself as a poet first, a politician only by accident, but though none of us was able to appreciate his Georgian verse the contrast between his demeanour and that of Kunitz was sufficient to establish that whereas the American lived precariously for verse the Georgian lived cosily as a member of the Soviet establishment.

Nevertheless Nonashvili was a charming and engaging companion. Walking along Rustaveli Boulevard with him one could understand how agreeable it must be to live in a small capital city where everyone knows you and you know everyone else. Our progress along the boulevard was marked with bows to right and left and raisings of the hat to friends strolling on the other side of the road. When Nonashvili asked whether we would prefer a Georgian or a European restaurant, we were nonplussed until he explained that 'European' meant Russian or French cooking while Georgian was strictly native, not only in cuisine but in customs. We saw what he meant as soon as we came down the steps of a cellar restaurant that had just opened in a narrow street planted with fruit trees in a distant quarter of the city. A Bacchanalian roar of singing welled out of the cellar. No women were present. ('Women do not go to national restaurants,' explained Nonashvili.) Waiters were hurrying to and fro with large earthenware jugs of wine like Greek amphorae. Some of the diners were eating shashlik but it was obvious that food played a minor part in the evening's enjoyment. The place was packed with men toasting one another in Homeric draughts of wine. There was not a table to be had, but friends of Nonashvili bobbed up on all sides competing for the honour of sharing their wine with foreigners. Terra-cotta mugs were pressed into our hands and we were urged to try the product of first one vineyard, then another, and it was obvious that if we could not find a table soon we could not reckon on being on our feet very long. An elderly gentleman who, Nonashvili told us, was a fellow deputy, presented Paul and me with a bottle of champagne apiece and a bar of chocolate which, I noticed, cost the equivalent of eight shillings. The din of toasting and of singing was so great one could hardly hear one's neighbour speak but after about half an hour of this high-pressure tippling we were relieved to be able to withdraw to a table in an adjoining room. Here we found a bonhomous gentleman with

TBILISI • Georgian Restaurant

long side whiskers in the act of declaring open a new wine bar. The wine lay in vats beneath the floor. In the centre of the room was a grotto and a fountain from which wine could gush forth and be caught in wooden stoops. The whiskery one turned out to be Vladimir Babkin, director of the All-Union Board of Foreign Tourism.

He appeared to be barely in his thirties and addressed us in fluent English.

''Ullo, 'ullo,' he boomed, 'what are a couple of cockneys doing in Tbilisi? The artist and the *homme de lettres* – what ho!'

'You look just like Peter Ustinov,' I said.

'My dear sir, I am extremely inebriated but I am definitely not an actor playing a part. I am what I am. Allow me to give you my card.'

And at the risk of falling into the fountain of wine he gave us a low bow and handed us a piece of pasteboard which imposingly set forth his responsibilities in Moscow. By this time we were quite as drunk as he was but though Georgian wine seems stronger than French it does not readily produce stupefaction but rather a sort of swelling euphoria which carries one onward and upward until sleep finally batters at the brain. Babkin was carrying his liquor with panache as though to say: 'Here's a Jew who can drink as deep as any Georgian and still be at his desk on time in the morning, which is more than you loose-living Caucasians can manage, I'll wager.'

We enjoyed Babkin's company but when we spoke of him later to the American attaché we were given what I have come to recognize in Russia as the standard American deflationary remark. 'Babkin? Oh yes, he's as shrewd as the proverbial cartload. Pops up in a variety of different jobs but there's not much doubt about his *real* profession – a four-letter man, if ever I saw one.'

The epithet is of course out-dated since the NKVD has now become the KGB, or State Security Commission. I could only reply: 'If you're right, they've raised the standard of recruitment since I was here last.'

Presently Babkin moved off to visit another restaurant (he was inspecting tourist resorts all over the country and urged us to give him our comments when we got back to Moscow) and we staggered out of the cellar into the anaesthetizing mountain air, only to burrow again into the Metro down the longest and steepest escalator I had ever been on. It is hard to believe that Tiflis really needs an underground railway; this one is only five miles long. Constructed at a great depth because of the mountainous terrain, it is replete with marble walls and crystal chandeliers like its parent in Moscow. I suppose they reckoned that Stalin's city must have a Metro, just as a matter of prestige.

*   *   *

Gori is not at all the simple mountain village I had expected but a fair-sized town, some sixty miles from Tiflis, the centre of a rich wine-growing district. Snow-capped mountains appear in the distance but Gori itself is flat and mundane, with broad streets, parks, a hotel and a busy bus terminal. Stalin's birthplace is a two-roomed wooden house which has been left on its original site while a park has been made around it. The house has been covered with a yellow marble building looking like a Moscow Metro station. Four large light globes on marble pillars have for no conceivable reason been placed on the roof. The overall effect is one of surpassing ugliness. Inside the house one of the rooms is furnished as it was at the time; the other, save for a few family photos, is bare. Perhaps the furniture of the second room was too poor to survive over the past seventy or eighty years. A photo of Stalin when young jogged my memory in an odd way. I placed my hand over the Georgian eyes and the rest of the face bore a strong resemblance to the Duke of Windsor as a schoolboy.

The Stalin Museum itself is well housed in a marble palace with rounded Georgian arches at ground level. The most interesting exhibits are his letter asking for admission to the Tiflis theological seminary and school reports setting out his examination results. There are a few touching letters to his daughter Svetlana and pictures of his domestic life with Alleluieva, the wife who committed suicide, and with friends such as Zhdanov. Considering that so much of his early life was spent in prison or in hiding, the number of youthful photographs is surprising. Many a prosperous young Englishman would not have been exposed to the camera so often: but many of the pictures were doubtless for the police gazette. There are many photostats of long-forgotten newspapers and a great many huge Gerasimov-style portraits showing him at all stages of his life, speaking to oil workers at Baku, escaping from Siberia and sometimes with Lenin on occasions when they were almost certainly never together. There is a roomful of official gifts such as royal personages receive; these are mainly ugly inkstands and ash-trays of modest cost. Records of his death and funeral have been added as an obvious afterthought. A death mask depicts him as shrunken and Oriental which he never was in life. The mourning crowds in Moscow and in cities abroad are shown in rather poorly framed newspaper cuttings. The Museum is a powerful reminder that Stalin was, after all, a Victorian and that the life recorded here belongs to an age that is past. Yet no attempt has been made to minimize the impact of what is now a unique tribute to his reputation. One cannot imagine anyone coming to Gori except to see the birthplace. I had been told that Gori was deserted, but this is not so. Motor coaches full of visitors kept arriving in the town and during the hour and a half that I spent at the birthplace at least fifty people went over the museum and a photographer with a tripod did a good trade at the door.

Since arriving in Georgia I had tried to resist the temptation to ask people I met what they thought of the most famous of all Georgians but after I had been to Gori my self-restraint broke down. The reply of some of the *Intourist* employees and strangers we met in the hotel was nearly always the same. 'Well, I suppose most people feel he was a great man who made mistakes.' I mentioned this to a young schoolteacher, a friend of Nonashvili's, who had been expatiating on the glory of the national poet, Shota Rustaveli, and said: 'For every hundred people in the West who know that Stalin was a Georgian I don't suppose more than one has even heard of Rustaveli.'

'That Stalin was a Georgian is not important to us,' he replied. 'True, most people now say he was a great man who made serious mistakes. But when mistakes are not only serious but very numerous, do they not then become crimes? For myself I don't believe in great men – no Borgias or Napoleons or Machiavellis for me. Mankind is better off without them.'

'I think you are talking with the benefit of hindsight,' I said. 'You must be too young to remember the building of socialism. Do you think it could have been done by Kosygin and Brezhnev and the sort of committee government you have now? I don't believe it could have been done at all in a backward country such as Russia was in the 'twenties without great leadership and this Stalin provided – no matter how heinous were his crimes later on. I am one who believes – not in heroes or human giants – but in the value and the rarity of exceptional men. Now that you have graduated as a great nation – recognized as such by all the world – you feel you can do without great men. But surely the likelihood is that you will produce more than you did before, though they will no doubt be very different in kind.'

'Personally,' said the schoolteacher, 'I have a great desire for a quiet life.'

And I thought to myself: 'Why can't I keep my big mouth shut? Why can't I leave my

GORi : the house where Stalin
was born Paul MOZ ARRA

Gori: Stalin's birthplace

"second country" alone – cease plotting its future course as though it were my fictional fatherland, Neurasthenia?'

★   ★   ★

Next morning we set off in two stout Volga cars for Kakhetia – Nonashvili, Paul and Kunitz in one car; the American attaché, another deputy and myself in the second. A heat haze hung over the city and out in the countryside we ran into a mist which slowed down our progress over the rough road. When it lifted a little we could see on each mountain top stone buildings that looked like churches but were really medieval watch-towers. A chain of them had been built from each frontier towards Tiflis: fires could be lit on each peak and so, in the same way as London received warning of the approach of the Spanish Armada, the Georgian monarchs could be informed that a frontier had been breached within thirty minutes.

'In the twelfth century,' said the deputy, 'our great Queen Tamara ruled over twenty million subjects: now we are only four and a half million but of course you will find Georgians all over the Soviet Union and most of them, I'm glad to say, are doing pretty well.'

'As well as the Armenians?' I asked.

'Perhaps not quite. They are the best business men in the world and we are not materialists. But in the arts and sciences, our performance is creditable.'

We drove for three hours through wide valleys containing rich farmland and many vineyards and then began a climb of 3,000 feet into the hills. A penetrating damp mist came down and the cars were reduced to a crawl, amid many jokes that we had brought one of our London fogs with us. At last we emerged into sunlight at the summit and found ourselves in the central square of Signachi, which could easily have been one of those hilltop villages in the country behind St. Tropez. It was in fact the county seat of a region containing some 60,000 people. We pulled up in front of the Communist Party headquarters where the local secretary was waiting to greet us. His relationship with Nonashvili seemed to be avuncular. Nonashvili referred all our questions to the secretary, explaining that having been a deputy only a few months he still had a lot to learn.

'Comrade Nonashvili has a great deal of homework to do!' declared the secretary, as he poured forth a stream of statistics about the fourteen collective farms and four State farms, the twenty-six day schools and three boarding schools that were in his charge. Nonashvili obediently sat taking a note of all that the secretary was saying. It was only when we moved into the secretary's dining-room where we were told 'Now we will have a few light refreshments – just a little breakfast' that the roles were reversed. Here Nonashvili the poet and townsman took over from the secretary who had just told us with pride that his father had been an illiterate farm worker. Nonashvili was soon on his feet making a speech of welcome, lauding the achievement of Stanley Kunitz in making Russian literature known to millions of Americans and even finding something felicitous to say about the American attaché whose role throughout Kunitz's tour was only that of a watch-dog. The 'breakfast', as we had feared, turned out to be a copious meal beginning with vodka and tomato soup and passing through the gamut of cold chicken and a variety of cheeses to end with ice cream and brandy.

Paul confided to me that all this seemed a form of cruelty to Kunitz, a man no longer young, who had been given this treatment all through White Russia and the Ukraine and had confessed that all he wished for now was a good cup of tea and a long sleep. I said that anyone who had read Churchill's *War Memoirs* ought to know that no one lacking a strong head and a good digestion should ever submit himself to Soviet hospitality.

When we moved off to visit a collective farm Nonashvili said that lest anyone think we were going to the best farm in the region we could select any farm we liked – even the worst. 'I'll bet each of the fourteen farms will be decked out in parade order,' said the American attaché *sotto voce*. 'They pull the same gag in the U.S. Army.' However, we selected a farm at random and were told that this happened to be the farthest away so we would not get back to Tiflis until the early hours. But, of course, we could not let this consideration deter us. And we were bound to admit that it was a very good farm indeed. A photograph of Stalin hung over the chairman's desk – the first we had seen in Russia. Called Zveli-Anaga, the farm covered 19,000 acres and comprised 2,500 people, of whom nearly half were registered as workers, There were 10,000 sheep, 1,300 cattle, 1,200 pigs and 16,000 hens. Over 500 acres were under vines and this provided the main profit. The average pay was 150 roubles a month, though shepherds and tractor drivers got as much as 250 roubles. Each homestead had an acre of land, mainly vineyard, from which one might expect 6 to 8 tons of grapes. A man and wife working on the collective together might average some 6,000 roubles a year, in addition to profits from their own plot.

The scope of these profits could be seen in the first homestead we went into. One thousand litres of white wine two years old lay in a vat beneath the cottage floor. An amphora was lowered into it and we were given drinks in wooden mugs. The man and his wife were at work so grandmother, aged eighty, did the honours. She produced goat cheese and a loaf of bread a yard long. She also bade us sample a pigskin full of newer wine suspended from the ceiling. Her house, like many others we passed, looked unfinished. The reason was that many families were building their own homes in their spare time; piles of bricks and roofing tiles lay in the yard to be added to the structure as opportunity allowed. These houses are now freehold and can be passed from father to son; all had electricity and running water but we saw no bathrooms and the sanitary arrangements were of the lean-to variety and stank as all the world must have stunk in the Dark Ages.

At the farm club house we were given copies of the collective farm newspaper – a fortnightly. Among the 'notes from abroad' the American attaché was delighted to find an item from his home town of Richmond, Virginia, recounting that 200 lb. of honey had been found inside a statue of Robert E. Lee when it was opened for repairs. The club house contained a full-sized theatre on the stage of which children were rehearsing for a dancing display. They wore traditional Georgian dress, the little girls in long lace skirts, and the music was provided by a harmonica band. Where, we asked, does the dancing master come from? He was not a farmer but lived in Signachi. It was a warm afternoon and the doors at the rear of the stage stood open, disclosing a green hillside brighter than the theatre lights and dotted with young lambs and grazing donkeys.

On a football field nearby we spoke with boys who had watched the World Cup games from England on Eurovision and who called their teams after the English players, Bobby Charlton and Bobby Moore.

In the evening we came to the house of an old peasant where the Signachi Party Committee had arranged to entertain us to dinner. The peasant presided at one end of his own table and Nonashvili at the other. Our host had been one of the first to join a collective and was now retired. His table was big enough to seat twenty guests and this was the number that now gathered around it. 'There's not been such a party here since my son was married,' said the old man. A little bewildered by this influx of foreigners, his poise was soon restored when Paul drew him aside for a portrait session. He had a marvellous head and when his turn came to raise a toast he spoke with dignity and well-mannered brevity.

The table was already laid with cold dishes when we reached it. The head of a piglet looked at me reproachfully, like the death mask of a baby. Then came mutton boiled in a broth of herbs with mint the prevailing taste, as in England. Shashlik of pork was served on spears, and the wine flowed as from a fountain, all of it produced on the collective, as was the brandy and the aquavit.

We were all given Georgian skull-caps to wear and very welcome they proved on the long night drive back to Tiflis when the mountain air struck cold. Kunitz took off the *beret* which never left his head and presented it to our host as a souvenir.

★   ★   ★

It was on our last day that we made contact with Nico Kiasashvili, who is reader in English literature at Tiflis University. A saturnine man who has often been in England, he feels a personal responsibility towards every English visitor but he had been out of town when we arrived.

'But this is appalling,' he exclaimed. 'You leave tomorrow, after only a few days, and I could have shown you so much! Who has been looking after you? What have you done?'

We told him and he was not impressed. 'Oh, this stupid peasant habit of pouring drink down the throats of foreigners until they can't see a thing! All sensible Georgians deplore it. It's not true hospitality – just silly exhibitionism. It's hard enough to get foreigners to spend time enough here to really understand us but if we make them drunk all the time, what can they possibly learn?'

We decided to spend a sober last evening in Nico's company. He called for us in his little Moskvich car and drove us up Mount Mtatsima past the church of St. David, the Pantheon of Georgian writers where Griboyedev, who married a Georgian woman and wrote the classic comedy *Wit Through Woe*, lies buried, to the park and restaurant at the summit. From here there is a splendid view over Tiflis to the glistening peaks of the high Caucasus many miles away. We ordered dinner on the terrace at the edge of the cliff. We surmised that Nico was not a rich man and asked him to be our guest but he would not have this and presently – even in his austere company – the Georgian hospitality he had deplored began to manifest itself in an unexpected manner which seemed to us more delicate and courteous than anything we had experienced before.

While we were waiting for our Shashlik Nico ordered a bottle of Napareouli, perhaps the best of the red wines, though he himself would drink only lemonade because he was driving on mountain roads. Some friends of his who were dining at a distant table waved to us and smiled and

presently two more bottles of Napareouli appeared on our table. Paul and I protested that we were again being overwhelmed with Georgian hospitality, the more so since our host was not drinking, and asked him if it would be thought rude if we declined to drink it. Nico explained that his friends at the distant table, seeing that he was entertaining some foreign guests, had inquired of the waiter what we were drinking and asked us to accept two more of the same with their best wishes. Ought we to go over to thank them or invite them to join us? we asked. Indeed no, we were told, that was not the custom. His friends did not wish to be intrusive, they had merely sent over the wine as a welcoming gesture; we might, if we wished, acknowledge the gift by raising our glasses to them and they would toast us in return but a more intimate exchange of courtesies was not called for. Now if we were only staying on a few days, a second meeting might be arranged . . .

'You see,' said Nico with assumed solemnity, 'Georgian hospitality is of two kinds and I hope you will find this type more acceptable.'

I told him I thought it was a highly civilized gesture and Paul and I, rising to our feet, silently toasted the distant friends, who rose and bowed to us in turn.

Nico spoke about his work. At the university he encouraged his students to avoid the obvious English texts and work on the arcane – for instance, William Golding. Until Nico wrote an article on Golding a couple of years earlier he had scarcely been heard of in Georgia but when the author visited Tiflis during the previous term he had been delighted to find that the students had taken him up and one girl actually presented a thesis on *Lord of the Flies*. Nico had translated a good deal of Shakespeare into Georgian and was now engaged upon *Ulysses*. *All* of it? we inquired in astonishment. Yes, the lot. He thought it would take him some five years. He had also considered attempting *Finnegans Wake* but because the Georgian language has no article and Joyce's book ends with the word 'the' he had thought better of it. I asked why he chose such an intractable author as Joyce. 'If I devote some of my life to making this obscure author comprehensible to our people,' he explained, 'perhaps some Irishman of genius will one day make Shota Rustaveli available to the English-speaking world. Most people think he's untranslatable but I believe it *could* be done. Look what that Englishman Fitzgerald did for Omar Khayyam!'

'Yes, but the Persians complain that Fitzgerald in effect took one of their minor poets and inflated him into an English classic while the major poets of Persia still remain unknown in the West.'

'That certainly wouldn't apply to Rustaveli – he *is* our greatest.'

Georgian peasant

Earlier in the evening I had observed, with a tourist's superficiality, that the Georgians seemed to me to be the Gascons of the Soviet Union. Now Nico built on that remark.

'Gascons we may appear when we say that Rustavelis is one of the great writers of all time, along with Shakespeare and Chaucer. We cannot prove it. No adequate translation exists into *any* other language. Rustaveli is a closed book even to Russians and in the wider world he can only be taken on trust. We know that very few non-Georgians will ever have time to learn our language and appreciate its riches as we do. So we must cry our wares, however boastful we may seem – no one else can do it for us.'

I attempted the consolatory argument that other small nations, notably Norway, had produced writers whose greatness had been recognized, even in poor translations, all over the world. If Georgia had an Ibsen, surely he could be made accessible?

'But we haven't got an Ibsen,' said Nico sadly. 'We are not advanced in the theatre. Our great period was the Middle Ages and every year that passes makes it more difficult to bridge the gap. I'll give you an English translation of *The Man in the Panther's Skin*, Rustaveli's greatest epic poem. It was written in the twelfth century but is perfectly comprehensible to every Georgian today; most of us in fact know much of it by heart. Parts of it may remind you of *The Song of Solomon*. It was meant to be sung to the harp of David, which probably came into the Caucasus with the Jews of the Babylonian captivity, and you may well wonder why, if it was possible to render *Solomon* into marvellous Renaissance English, the same could not be done for Rustaveli. This English translation is, of course, only a literal one – the essence of the poem just isn't there.'

Nico left us with a melancholy impression of what it must be like to be a highly erudite citizen of a small nation, well-versed in the literature of Western Europe and of Russia yet isolated by the barrier of language from what ought to be a full cultural exchange on level terms. I had recently seen at the Curzon Cinema in London a short Georgian feature film which had charmed me. Nico had seen it too. 'An excellent film,' he said. 'But how many Englishmen can have noticed it was made in the streets of Tiflis? It was a charade, remember? From start to finish, the actors never spoke.'

Symptomatic, I wondered, of how Georgians see themselves today? A nation of mummers, who communicate only in mime because their true essence is locked up in a language which the world has passed by?

Nico went on sipping his lemonade. Two more bottles of Napareouli appeared on the table, accompanied by bars of Georgian chocolate. A second group of Nico's friends were paying their compliments to his guests and Paul and I rose once more to mime our thanks and to receive a silent acclamation in return. Words would in any case have been superfluous because an orchestra was now playing and an elderly singer – 'his voice has cracked,' said Nico, 'but at seventy-three years of age he's still one of the best folk singers we have' – was giving us an old Georgian ballad which reduced some of our fellow-diners to tears.

Paul MAZARBA : Udarnik movie theatre

Cinema of the 'twenties

Kiev: Dom Gorodetskogo

Kiev: Art Nouveau mansion

6 KIEV

From Tiflis to Kiev we took the big Tupolev jet again – the aircraft which serves the international routes. This one connected Erevan in Armenia with Tiflis, Kiev and Leningrad and then went on to Archangel. There was only just time in the two hours and twenty minutes we were airborne for the single hostess to serve breakfast to some eighty passengers. The Borispol airport at Kiev possessed the most functional terminal building we had yet seen and was well supplied with restaurants and shops. Paul and I bought what appeared to be the best bargain we had yet encountered – some Romeo and Julietta cigars which worked out at rather less than a shilling each. But there was a snag. The boxes had never seen a humidor since they left Havana and the cigars had the consistency of hay and were almost unsmokeable though, having nothing better, we smoked them all in time.

The highway into Kiev runs broad and straight between tall trees like a good *route nationale* in France: well-tended woods and orchards lie on either side and the cottages are large and built of brick. The Ukrainian character may be as 'wide' as the Russian but in building and in husbandry more attention seems to be paid to neatness and clean line than in Russia proper. The freshly gilded domes of the great Pechersk Monastery soon came into view on the high escarpment above the Dnieper river on which the city is built. The Dnieper is a noble stream 1000 feet wide and laced by many bridges. Hydrofoil ships driven by jet engines were plying on the river. Kiev is splendidly sited on thickly wooded cliffs which have never been built over. One is reminded of the

Samarkand: the mausoleums of Shah-i-Zinda

Leas at Folkestone, though on a far larger scale, for at the base of the escarpment there are bathing beaches, as though the great river were a sea, and the islands in the stream are also reserved for swimming and boating. I was surprised to find the city so completely healed after all it had suffered in the war. The main thoroughfare, Khreshchatik, was, of course, laid in ruins and has been entirely rebuilt, inevitably in the most voluptuous Stalin style, but the scale of destruction elsewhere cannot have been as bad as one had supposed at the time for, apart from the Uspensky Cathedral which was deliberately blown up by the Germans, the whole Pechersk complex of churches and monasteries is intact, the blue and white baroque church of St. Andrew and the charming little imperial palace, both designed by Rastrelli, are as good as new; the crimson-painted university with its 17,000 students has been fully restored, the Taras Shevchenko house has not been damaged at all and the splendid boulevard named after the poet remains as fine as anything Baron Haussmann laid out in Paris. The great area of parkland along the Dnieper makes Kiev more truly a garden city than any other I know. One can stroll about the centre of the city with plenty of shade above one's head; the noise and bustle of Moscow are entirely absent and at times it is difficult to believe that 1,300,000 people really live in this sylvan place. The secret of Kiev's viability is rigorous town-planning which has preserved the city centre as it was laid out in the late eighteenth and early nineteenth centuries while building what amounts to a new city on the other side of the river. It is the recent construction of an underground railway which has really made this possible. The Metro emerges from its tunnel on the river bank at the base of the cliff on which the city stands and is then carried across the Dnieper by a new bridge to serve the industrial and residential area on the further bank. Already 250,000 people live in the new town and most of them work in plants nearby so that commuting across the river is kept in check. But it is the central escarpment which still counts. Here stands the new Pioneers' Palace built in the same style as the Palace of Congresses at Moscow. Here is situated the monument to Prince Vladimir at whose instigation the people of Kiev were baptized as Christians in the Dnieper in the year 988; here too is the grave of the unknown soldier over which an eternal flame burns and whence solemn music wells out of the ground upon each hour, and here stands the monument to General Vatutin, who was mortally wounded when recapturing Kiev in April 1944, and also the graves of thirty-four of his officers who fell in the battle. Most of them seem to have been Colonels barely forty years of age. Not far off is the Sports Stadium which was due to open on 21 June 1941 but, for reasons which seemed good at the time, never did. When its ruined shell was rebuilt after the war all holders of invitations to the opening who were still alive were told that their tickets would be honoured – an episode that reminded me of the immortal first sentence with which the late *Daily Mirror* writer Cassandra reopened his column after six years of war – 'As I was saying when I was so rudely interrupted . . .'

Perched high on the escarpment too, at the foot of Khreshchatik, is the new Dnipro Hotel where we stayed. The walls on our floor were pale green with doors painted crushed raspberry. The rooms were small and somewhat American. There was TV on every landing (mainly used by football fans) and two tiny lifts served the twelve storeys. Only one worked at a time with the result that sad human crocodiles wound their way up and down the stairs.

I had an introduction to Alexei Poltoratsky, a journalist friend of my old colleague Alexander Werth, who very hospitably whisked me off to the opera at short notice. So short was it indeed that Paul got left behind. He had discovered a staggering *art nouveau* mansion in a chestnut-shaded street just behind the hotel and on ascertaining that it had been built by a Ukrainian sugar baron as a memorial to his daughter who had gone down in the *Titanic*, determined to record forthwith the writhing sea-serpents, the recumbent mermaids and other denizens of the deep which the poor young lady must be presumed to have encountered in her watery grave – all delineated on the façade in concrete very much as sugar icing is piped onto a cake. Poltoratsky himself worked in a slightly less exotic but rather similar mansion dating from the 'nineties which had belonged to the family of General Ignatiev, an old Tsarist officer of my acquaintance who soldiered on in the Red Army. He really came into his own in the second World War when Stalin appointed him to brush up the *mores* of the officer corps when it became clear that they would soon be making their first appearance in Central Europe since their encounter with Marshal Pilsudski in the 'twenties. Ignatiev ran an institution that was known as 'the dancing academy' where he and his wife, who had been a ballerina, gave lessons in deportment and etiquette. And at Kremlin functions they would appear together, both wearing white gloves, he bowing over the hands of the ladies in a manner that was probably fashionable when Stalin was a boy but which had long since disappeared in the West. Poltoratsky told me he felt on the same wavelength as Ignatiev because he too had married a ballerina. Enormously tall and broadshouldered, Poltoratsky looks like a Cossack officer but is in fact the son of a Jewish intellectual who wrote novels in Yiddish. Mrs. Poltoratsky used to dance in the Kharkov Ballet and they have been married for thirty years. When we took our seats in the front row of the stalls to see *The Fountain of Bakshi-serai*, Mrs. Poltoratsky complained that we were far too close to appreciate the ballet. Why hadn't her husband insisted on being placed farther back?

'Mr. Jacob is seated in the place of honour,' he replied. 'Stolypin, the Prime Minister, occupied that very seat one night in 1911, with the Tsar up there in the imperial box, at a gala performance to celebrate the three hundredth anniversary of the Romanov dynasty. Bogrov the anarchist, who was also said to be an agent of the secret police, shot and mortally wounded Stolypin as he sat there. Every one thought he would then assassinate the Tsar but he meekly gave himself up. A very odd night's work.'

I looked over my shoulder to where the assassin had been sitting and gazed into the face of Tim Buck, the old Canadian Communist who was dreamily listening to the overture in the midst of a delegation from Toronto. *Autres temps, autres moeurs.*

'I still think we'd be better off farther back,' said my hostess.

In the interval Poltoratsky told me a story which he said he still found incredible but which had actually happened to him at Stalingrad. As a German-speaking officer, he had to interrogate prisoners as soon as they were rounded up and among a group of German officers who came out of a bunker with their hands in the air he noticed one fairly cheerful character who approached him and held out his hand.

'I do not shake hands with Germans,' said Poltoratsky, whereupon the officer asked if he might speak to Poltoratsky privately in English.

'There was something about the man that intrigued me,' said Poltoratsky, 'so I took him aside and he then said to me with the greatest urgency: "You may not believe me but I am a member of the British intelligence service. Here is my number. Please ask your colonel to contact the British Military Attaché in Moscow immediately; tell him I have come over and he will confirm the truth of what I say for he is expecting me. Please make haste for as you can imagine I have news of the greatest importance which cannot wait." '

'What did you do?'

'I believed the man. I telephoned headquarters who thought I was out of my mind but they sent an escort and the fellow was taken away. Later my colonel told me that the British Embassy had been informed and that the man was being flown to Moscow. But, you know how it is in war, one never hears the end of any story. Was the man an impostor? If he was not, and is still alive, perhaps he will read this story and will write to you. If he does – please let me know. I would like to apologize for not shaking his hand.'

Poltoratsky struck me as decidedly anglophile, perhaps because he edits the magazine *Czecvit* which has published in Ukrainian William Golding's *Lord of the Flies*, *Cakes and Ale* and *Theatre* by Somerset Maugham, Arnold Wesker's *Chips with Everything* and, as he said, 'as much as we could manage of Joyce's *Ulysses*'. I thought it unlikely that he had 'managed' Molly Bloom's soliloquy but felt it unfair to twit him on this point.

'English writers have always been popular with us,' he said. 'For historical reasons, I think. Ever since Napoleon we've seen that in times of mortal danger the English and the Russians always come together. And so Englishmen – no matter how far apart we are in political life – are always welcome here because our people know that our basic interests are the same.'

He was interesting about the development of the Ukrainian language. 'In our Writers' Union,' he said, 'we have seven hundred members, most of whom write in Ukrainian although some use Yiddish, Russian, Polish or Hungarian, and one might think this is a damned sight too many when one considers that the entire Russian literature of the nineteenth century was created by fifteen men at most. But there's a great linguistic renascence here and one must take that into account. After all, in Tsarist times Ukrainian was virtually forbidden: Kiev was completely Russianized and not a single school taught in Ukrainian. We had about sixty thousand folk songs, but popular choirs were allowed to perform them only in French.'

'Why was this,' I asked, 'when the Polish language flourished?'

'Because the Tsar was Tsar of all the Russias, and King of Poland. But the Ukraine was not allowed a separate identity – even as Finland was – because its great wealth was thought to be a standing temptation to other European powers, as we know it was to Germany. Enforced Russianization, though, was the most imbecile way of making people loyal to the Tsar. However, the net result was that our language was artificially stunted for generations despite the fact that in Taras Shevchenko we produced a giant of world literature. Shevchenko was a serf who wrote verse in Ukrainian but was obliged to use Russian for his prose, or he would never have been published. He was actually bought out of serfdom by Russian aristocrats who perceived his genius. He was exiled to the Caspian Sea for ten years and forced to serve in the Army but here again liberal Russian officers spotted his great talent as a painter and saw to it that he had time to pursue his second art. Although he returned from exile a broken man he lived to become an

Academician. He was the real creator of the modern Ukrainian language; that was why they persecuted him. The cities being completely Russified, the language was kept alive only in the villages and Shevchenko was a peasant genius. You know, Louis Aragon was quite right when he pointed out that there's really no such thing as "Russian literature". The literature of our country is multi-lingual and this certainly creates difficulties. For example, I don't use Yiddish any more: I consider myself a Ukrainian and I write in that language. I read Russian, of course, and manage a bit of Byelorussian – but that's all. I've been on holiday in a Georgian village where I actually had to use sign language – no use talking to me about Rustaveli, I don't even know his alphabet. And once I met some Caucasian writers from a small autonomous republic down there who always addressed each other in Russian. And when I said, why don't you use your own tongue? they replied, "Well, which one? We have six different languages and God knows how many dialects so Russian has to be our lingua franca." '

About living conditions in Kiev Poltoratsky was emphatic. 'I wouldn't live anywhere else – it's a glorious city – but then I'm a very fortunate man. I've only published one novel but it sold well: I made fourteen thousand roubles out of it and you know, a writer doesn't pay more than thirteen per cent in income tax so that gave me a good start. Then I have a flat in the centre – four rooms, with only three in the family – and my rent is nine roubles a month. With gas, electricity, heating and telephone, say a bit under thirty roubles altogether. But naturally a great many people live nothing like so well. Housing is still a very hard and complex problem. Before the war there were eight hundred thousand Kievites: two hundred thousand were killed and two hundred and fifty thousand transported to Germany and the population that remained has trebled. You can see we've built almost a new city but it's far from being sufficient. A few years back only five per cent of our people had a flat of their own – everyone else had to share baths and kitchens. The backlog of bad housing is enormous.'

When I got back to the hotel a small crowd was admiring a luxurious motor coach parked outside which was labelled 'Moscow–Nice via Warsaw & Vienna'. Most of them assumed it was foreign until they spotted the su number plate and the inscription *Gaz* on the bonnet and exclaimed with pride: 'One of ours.'

I found Paul in the dining-room. He had been picked up by a group of art students who had found him sketching in the Pechersk Monastery. They had taken him to a wine bar and insisted on standing him glasses of wine and pickled cucumbers with the result that after two or three

Kiev: the Pechersk Monastery

hours Paul was more than ready for a real meal. But he had reckoned without the obstructive technique of a female restaurant boss dressed in a variant of the male dinner jacket whom we christened Gloria Updyke. This lady had at her disposal a team of tremendously plump Wagnerian waitresses who – left to themselves and without the stimulus of a tip – would no doubt have been pleased to serve us. But Miss Updyke – who perhaps doubled the roles of *maître d'hôtel* and shop steward? – insisted on their working to rule and as soon as one of them seemed inclined to respond to our beckoning fingers she would whisk her off for an hour's meal break. Whenever the service doors swung open one could see these ladies seated in the wings, tucking in to fragrant bowls of bortsch while we, the paying customers, languished under the chandeliers without even a roll to play with. After three-quarters of an hour of this treatment an Afghan student who was sharing our table uttered an infuriated ululating cry which in his native mountains might well have signalized the massacre of a whole tribe. Miss Updyke bore down upon him with a severe expression and said: 'Complaining again, citizen? Please show some patience: all countries have their failings and perhaps your own is not without blemish.'

I learned that the failing she was referring to was not so much impatience as speculation for it is popularly supposed that many of the oriental and African students at Soviet universities receive black market roubles purchased abroad through their embassies and that this enables them to live in luxury at the expense of the Soviet treasury. (This alleged practice also annoys the United States Embassy which has to pay 15 roubles (£6) a night for an hotel room for any visiting national, being too scrupulous to import black currency.) The Afghan, though a veritable wolf cub in appearance, accepted the rebuke with humility, even though we were finally served before him. But he cemented these suspicions by asking us whether life was very dear in London. When we told him it was cheaper than in Paris and that he could purchase a return excursion from B.E.A. in roubles he said: 'In that case I could live *en prince* in London for I have many roubles.' Speculation in currency, or selling the rouble short, is of course a serious offence under Soviet law and carries a long term of imprisonment.

I was reminded of the Press tycoon who offered me £800 a year to become his correspondent in Moscow in 1939 and when I asked for more, declared: 'But my dear young man, you'll get all your roubles on the black market and live like a fighting cock!' This was a measure of the supercilious attitude many supporters of Chamberlain's appeasement policy – and this tycoon was a leader of the pack – still adopted towards Russia at that time. Yet how outraged they would have been to hear that Tass or the Associated Press had sent a chief correspondent to London with instructions to live and run his bureau on smuggled currency. No doubt my tycoon thought I was throwing away the chance of a lifetime when I rejected his offer and went to France as a war correspondent instead. But at a better time and on a proper salary Lord Beaverbrook sent me to Russia four years later and I never had cause to regret the delay.

'Are ya happy with me? Do I pay ya enough?' he once inquired in his well-known prosecuting attorney voice.

And injudiciously – for he did not relish liturgical jokes – I replied: 'You are the only Lord I know whose service is perfect freedom.'

But, returning to the Wagnerian waitresses, Paul found them socially significant. 'Tough as old boots,' he said, 'but think how they'd look after you if you had one of them all to yourself.'

There were many more such Brunnhildes at the Darnitsya textile plant which I went to visit next morning. Nearly 70 per cent of the workers together with the managing director and the trade union organizer are women. The plant did not exist before the war. It was the first factory built in the new town across the river in 1947: still incomplete, it already employs 8,000 workers, one third of whom work a night shift. The Party Secretary of the plant, Pavel Stepanovich Mikhailchuk, had been an electrician until he got the Party post a year before. Like most young Party officials one meets in Russia he struck me as being extremely able, with an encyclopaedic knowledge of every process, every social trend within the plant.

'Our chief problem,' he said, 'is not the factory itself, though it was built in a hurry and needs a good deal of modernization, but the social organization. You see our girls keep on having babies and that means more and more kindergartens because without these we can't expect women to come to work.'

He took me to see one of them. There are ten in all with not more than 140 children in each and they are run on lavish lines. Yet another Wagnerian lady, a Siberian named Nina Zyelkova, was in charge of the one I visited. She declared that the cost of food per month was 70 roubles for each child. The best-paid parents paid no more than 12.50 a month for each child and the lower paid only 6 or 4 roubles so the factory had to put up a considerable sum in addition to the State grant towards expenses. Each kindergarten has a resident woman doctor and a large staff of cooks and teachers. The one I saw was as clean as a hospital and lavishly equipped with toys and children's furniture. It was in fact a nursery such as no Russian child could match at home and one could imagine a woman going to work at Darnitsya not only to add some 120 roubles a month to the family income but mainly so that her child should spend its days during the first seven years of life in such gracious surroundings.

The factory itself struck me as unremarkable. One or two shops were air-conditioned and filled with modern Soviet machinery: others were appallingly noisy and running on older machines from England, Japan, Czechoslovakia and Italy. But then I am allergic to factory life. No matter how advanced may be the principles under which it is organized, the basic process of mass production seems to me brutish and nasty. Mikhailchuk was frankly shocked when I told him this was the first textile plant I had ever been in. 'And you from England – the motherland of textiles!' he remonstrated. I said that to me one factory looks very like another and to spend one's life minding a machine in such a place – even one from which all 'exploitation' had been removed – seemed to me a deprivation of liberty. I told him that the English writer Ford Madox Ford had suggested some forty years ago that it was quite wrong that factories should be manned by any one segment of society. Everyone, Ford argued, ought as a social duty to spend a certain proportion of his life working in a factory – authors, artists, civil servants, doctors, lawyers and so on. Ford believed that although industrialization was essential for every society aspiring to lead the good life, industrial work was in essence so soul-destroying that it ought to be shared out by all, just as military service is a duty for all. Of course Ford had not foreseen the arrival of automation in our lifetime.

'Aha,' said Mikhailchuk, 'and that is where I think the English Mr. Ford is out-dated. We know here that automation is coming quite soon. Our problem is not how to induce more people to share the work but how to provide all the leisure activities our staff will require when full automation arrives. We've just gone over to the five-day week but before very long we shall have machinery that really runs itself: we shan't want machine-minders then, only more highly paid engineers and of course maintenance men to keep it all running. Even so, a smaller staff will earn a basic income within a very short working week and will be free to take up other activities for the rest of the time. What should these activities be? that is the question. Sport? Study? perhaps a second profession altogether? These are very big questions which we are beginning to study now because before very long they will be calling for solution. As of now, I don't mind telling you, we don't know the answers.'

Tsarskoe Selo: the Chinese village

Leningrad: the artists' necropolis

7 LENINGRAD

A deflating remark which irks many a traveller returned from the Soviet Union is the perennial: 'I don't suppose you actually met many *Russians*?'

Considering the short time we spent in each place and the fact that on most days Paul was working in the open air from morning till night, I think it true to say that we met as many natives as we would have done in any other country. Nor were these natives retiring: many were voluble to an embarrassing degree and had Paul and I spoken Russian as we would have wished to do, we could have spent all our time discussing the state of the world with Soviet citizens.

In Kiev, friends and colleagues of Alexei Poltoratsky came forward at short notice to entertain us and try out their English, when they had any. Marc Pinchevsky, a translator of English books into Ukrainian, possessed the best knowledge of current English literature of any Russian I had yet met. He explained this by saying that since he could not handle work which was already available in Russian, he had to search the highways and byways of English writing to find books that were worth producing for the Ukrainian public alone. Vladimir Gusev, a young man who had spent four years in the Soviet trade delegation in Egypt, was curious to compare Nasser's Egypt with the country I had known under the ample rump of King Farouk. Mrs. Kolosova, the president of the Ukrainian Friendship Society, apologized for not having us to dinner because she was just off on a visit to England, but Igor Kazimirov made up for this by escorting us all over town and providing a car for us whenever we needed one. Kazimirov, a rotund and bonhomous

Leningrad: the Rostral Column

character, insisted on driving us to the airport at six o'clock in the morning to catch the plane to Leningrad. He gave us a breakfast of garlic sausages and coffee in the airport bar and then took so many pictures of us in the neighbouring gardens that we had to ask him whether they were really for his own album or for the police files.

'I am a great camera fan,' he replied. ' I take pictures all the time when I have a good subject.'

We observed that he bore some resemblance to Winston Churchill and gave him one of our infamous Kiev cigars to make the impersonation more convincing. He stuck the cigar in his mouth and struck some Churchillian poses against the background of aircraft on the tarmac while we recorded his antics with his own camera.

'Kazimirov taking off for a summit conference of celestial bodies on Venus,' he declared, while we expressed our admiration for such high spirits so early in the morning.

When the time came for us to emplane his camera followed us all the way up the steps and then, after we had waved goodbye, he implored us to step down again. Something had been forgotten. It turned out to be a big Ukrainian embrace on both cheeks. The outcome of this exuberant leave-taking was that we were received on the plane with unaccustomed deference. Crew and passengers had received the impression that we were very important persons indeed.

In Leningrad, as elsewhere, we tried to steer clear of official personages as much as possible but we had been advised not to miss the 'friendship house' there because, in the true Leningrad tradition, it was not a house at all but a splendid palace. And so we found it – a palatial building facing the Fontanka Canal, dating from 1790 and containing a ballroom and reception rooms decorated in scarlet, ivory and gold and a marble staircase on the scale of Lancaster House in London.

The existence of these 'friendship houses' in all the main cities is a development I applaud, though they will certainly be regarded askance by those visitors who regard every Party-inspired activity with suspicion. It is true that they are a convenient way of channelling contacts with foreigners through one centre but the Russians who frequent these places are by no means all Party stalwarts; very many of them, I would guess, are non-Party professional or artistic people who join the affiliated societies for promoting exchanges with England, France, Latin America or the Arab world because their interests lie in a particular direction, or merely because they enjoy social contacts with foreigners or hope to use the societies as stepping-stones towards travelling abroad themselves. Most of the work done by the Russian members is on a voluntary, spare-time basis. Few Russians even now have the means or the space to entertain foreign visitors in their own homes and the houses are a substitute for the drawing-rooms and salons of the West. To the foreigner, they are an invaluable means of making contacts. An English doctor or scientist arriving in Leningrad, for instance, could meet Russian specialists in his own field more quickly through the palace on the Fontanka than by calling at hospitals or learned societies himself. When we telephoned the palace on arrival we were put on to a young intern in a Leningrad hospital, Dr. Drogachev, who called in at our hotel on his way home from work, inquired what we wanted to do over a drink with us and undertook to tell the people we wanted to see that we were in town. As an amateur public relations officer, the doctor was hardly a ball of fire. Many of his inquiries bore no fruit partly, no doubt, on account of the appalling telephone service but mainly because the young man was exceedingly overworked and seemed on the verge of a nervous breakdown.

When we met him the next day he apologized for his lack of efficiency and confessed that he was so tired he could hardly get through the working day. However, he managed to find some of the addresses and telephone numbers we wanted and these were enough to give us a full programme.

We went to tea with Mrs. Elena Petrova, who has written a book on Byron based on material she gathered at Cambridge. She had spent some months there on a grant and had not wasted her time for her knowledge of our life and language was far from superficial. She was a rumbustious blonde woman with a strong, teasing personality and her grown-up son seemed in awe of her. Another guest from whose donnish personality this formidable lady extracted the mickey was Yuri Kuznets, a lecturer at the Leningrad Institute of Technology who asked if he might call on us when he paid his first visit to England in the following summer. Kuznets was thirty-five and very English in appearance with a soft brown moustache. He complained of being unable to cope with domestic life while his wife was away on holiday and Mrs. Petrova suggested that he should clear the tea-table of its remaining doughnuts and take them home for his supper. But Kuznets was soaring above the doughnut level. He informed us that his favourite English authors were James Aldridge, A. L. Morton and, as he said, 'Herbert Wells'. Among academics, he liked Maurice Dobb and the Master of Balliol, Christopher Hill. Learning that Aldridge and I were old friends, he deplored the fact that Aldridge is not a leading figure in English letters for, as he reminded us, he is considered in Russia to be a major novelist. He was also concerned to know who is better informed about the other's country – the Englishman or the Russian? I thought that while many English intellectuals are passionately interested in Russia, the man in the street . . .

'The man on the Clapham omnibus,' interposed Mrs. Petrova, and I bowed my acknowledgments . . .

. . . has a vague feeling of benevolence, perhaps of indebtedness, since Russia's losses in the war were so much greater than ours, but has no special desire to find out more. And, I added, one is astonished that some Russians know as much about England as they do for if one was to read *Pravda* or *Izvestia* for year after year one would discover almost nothing. These papers, for one thing, are too small to attempt proper coverage in the same way as *The Times* man in Washington, for instance, tries to tell the story of America from one day to the next.

To this Kuznets replied: 'We have other sources' and he produced from his briefcase a new magazine of international affairs which, he declared, had serialized Anthony Eden's memoirs and habitually gave the texts of speeches by Harold Wilson and Edward Heath. But when we came to examine the issue, the evidence was inconclusive for this was a special May Day number, filled with the usual eulogies of Lenin.

While the ordinary Russian who wanted to inform himself about England would hardly know where to begin – apart from listening to the BBC, of course – the Leningrad intellectuals whom we met proved to be reasonably well informed. We looked up an old acquaintance of Paul's, a professor of art named Valentine Brodsky. We went to the Union of Artists to meet some of his friends and to see an exhibition of his prints. This had ended a few days earlier but was reopened for our benefit. Brodsky looks like an English colonel with a clipped grey moustache. He went through the war unscathed all the way from the Volga to the Spree with a copy of Kipling's poems in his knapsack but when he got to Berlin he lost them. So now he wanted to know if we could send him a paperback Kipling from London. With him we went to spend the evening at the home of Vladimir Galba, the caricaturist, and his wife Anna Teterevnikova. They have an agreeably old-fashioned apartment on the Street of the Decembrists. A single tramline runs down the centre of the street and the houses have tall shuttered windows and high-ceilinged rooms: there is even a shallow stone staircase and a concierge in the courtyard to remind one of Paris. Apartments such as these have known absolutely no change since the revolution. Mrs. Galba is of Dutch origin – and she was packing up before going to the Netherlands for a month's holiday. There were old family pictures on the walls and on Mrs. Galba's desk lay a large manuscript.

This was her translation of one of George Sand's novels which are being brought out in a new collected edition.

'You may think it rather old-fashioned,' she said, 'but there's quite a revival of Sand going on here. She is very popular among young people, oddly enough.'

I said that in several countries the young seemed to be swinging back to long-outmoded enthusiasms. In England the Beatles had rediscovered the cult of the lotus and the navel – oblivious of the fact that sixty years before superannuated *memsahibs* from India had aroused general merriment by their dalliance with Hindu mysticism.

We sat at a round table drinking vodka with cheese and ham on toast followed by coffee and a home-made cake. And we discovered that the most recent recipients of Mrs. Galba's hospitality had been Canon Collins of St. Paul's Cathedral and his wife, together with a former editress of *Vogue*. Vladimir Galba has a remarkable collection of the history of comic art including volumes on Paul's forebear, William Hogarth – everything, in fact, from the horrific satire of Hieronymus Bosch through *Punch* and *Simplicissimus* down to the drawings of Gerald Scarfe. To me the most fascinating items were the bound volumes of the Petersburg journal *Satirikon* which reached its apogee in 1910. This paper poked fun at Tsarist bureaucracy in a style which *Krokodil* seems to have inherited. Without being overtly political, it managed to convey the general backwardness of Russia by depicting the rich either as gross lechers or as corseted nancy boys. The poor made no appearance in this Russo–Victorian *Private Eye* except as coachmen, serving wenches or beggars. The advertisements of *Satirikon* were nuggets of pickled history. They included *art nouveau* colophons for the court jeweller Fabergé: on our way to the Galbas' we had searched vainly through a foreign currency trinket shop for some presents to take home only to notice on our way out that the customary drab name plate had been removed to reveal underneath a marble plaque engraved in Latin script, *Fabergé*.

★   ★   ★

Dr. Drogachev and the Galbas were kind enough to introduce me to one of the curators of the Hermitage, Mrs. Kroll, who has spent forty years as a Keeper of English Art in the museum. Mrs. Kroll comes from an old Petersburg family of German origin. 'We left our mark in Berlin,' she said, 'in the form of the Kroll Opera House.' But when I asked what were her feelings when the Germans arrived in the suburbs of Leningrad she said she was thankful to have been spared the siege, for she and her precious pictures had been evacuated to Central Asia where they spent the entire war. Mrs. Kroll's special care is the collection which Catherine the Great bought from the estate of Horace Walpole and she also showed me the magnificent Rembrandt rooms and the galleries of modern French masters which are housed on the top floor of the Winter Palace in what had formerly been the bedrooms of the Tsarina's ladies-in-waiting. Here can be seen no fewer than 31 Picassos, 27 Matisses, 10 Cézannes, 6 Gauguins and a number of Van Goghs, not to mention innumerable examples of Derain, Modigliani, Marie Laurencin and others of the School of Paris.

The galleries of the Hermitage cover more than nine acres. Mrs. Kroll told me I could not hope to see them all in less than a week and when I told her I had only one day to spend there I felt I no longer had the right to mock at the jet-packaged American tourist. Even a few hours in the Hermitage sent me back to the Astoria Hotel with sagging knees.

A charming woman from the Leningrad evening paper came to interview us. She bore the stately name of Ivetta Nikolaevna Knazieva and she was not just neatly dressed, she was positively chic. I told her what a pleasure it was to hear her beautiful Russian (Petersburg style) – so clear and quick-spoken, as though it were French – after the laborious provincial and oriental accents we had listened to on our travels. Leningraders of the old school derive this, I am sure, from having learned French as their first language, and the accent has been handed down from parent to child, but oddly enough only in the female line. The masculine Petersburg accent as spoken in the *corps des pages* and in Guards regiments under the Empire was a sort of anglicized drawl which is now preserved only by a few elderly exiles and by my friend Alexander Werth, who was born and educated in St. Petersburg. Madame Knazieva was, I think, pleased by my compliment but she did her best not to show it for her approach as an interviewer had nothing of the *ancien régime* about it. She plied us with intelligent questions about our tour and then came a question which I felt sure had been set by her news editor: 'What message have you got for the people of Leningrad on their May Day holiday?'

We were both completely stumped by this.

'I know what news editors are,' I said at last. 'But I can't possibly answer that. Living as I do in a hideous quarter of London called Battersea, I could of course ask Leningraders if they realize how damned lucky they are to be living in one of the most beautiful cities in the world. Or I could

'Leningrad – streets open at the Maly Theatre'

express the hope that the Soviet Government will get around to finding a *use* for this city which will be in some measure worthy of it. After the war I remember there was talk of Leningrad becoming the capital of the RSFSR while Moscow remained the national capital. But it seems that Leningrad remains just the second city in size while its splendours serve no particular purpose.'

Madame Knazieva's pencil remained poised over her notebook. This was not at all what her editor wanted.

'We Leningraders feel,' she said, 'that our city doesn't *need* any political up-grading. We are so proud of it as it is.'

'Come, Madame. Let's talk off the record for a moment. Everyone must agree that Lenin was perfectly right to move the capital back to Moscow. The Communist Party does somehow fit into the atmosphere of the Kremlin, which is a national shrine, whereas it would *not* have found an appropriate home in a city built by autocrats to house an imperial government. But your city is like Rome, one of the architectural glories of the world and the birthplace of Russian literature as well. If you can find no substitute for the role it played during two centuries, isn't there a danger of its becoming just a museum?'

'I can only say that we who live here are not worried by this thought,' said Madame Knazieva.

If I lived in Leningrad, I would not merely be worried, I would eventually be driven into living somewhere else. The atmosphere of the imperial city is, even today, so powerful that to my mind it entirely eclipses the modern Soviet city which has grown up around it, reducing the Soviet people who live in it – more civilized and pleasant though they be, perhaps, than the inhabitants of any other Soviet city – to a state of irrelevance, of virtual non-being. As one contemplates the enormous vistas of classical architecture one feels that the tiny contemporary figures thinly spread across them have no business to be here at all. All contemporary Russian books about Leningrad devote much space, of course, to establishing it as the City of Lenin. It is true that Lenin lived and worked here, albeit briefly, and that all the great revolutionary events occurred here. But in scrupulously preserving the imperial city in all its splendour, the Soviet Government has through its very artistic integrity given the game away. For it is not the spirit of Lenin that broods here, it is the spirit of the Romanov dynasty, of the growing might over two centuries of the Russian Empire and the flowering of Russian literature and art in the nineteenth century. Had Prince Lvov or Kerensky triumphed over Lenin, it is conceivable that Petersburg might

Tsarskoe Selo:
the Cameron Gallery

have become the worthy capital of a bourgeois republic. But a new world was born here and it simply does not fit into the glorious fabric of the old. The vigorous, talented and kindly people of Leningrad claim this city as their own. But it was not made for them. It was never intended to be a part of the century of the Common Man.

★   ★   ★

All this was not so obvious when I first came here twenty-three years ago, for Leningrad then had narrowly escaped total destruction. The siege, in which upwards of 650,000 people had died of starvation, had recently been lifted. The Germans were in full retreat but the Finns were still standing firm only fifteen miles from the city. All the ruined buildings were thickly mantled in snow, the temperature was 12° below zero Fahrenheit and very little glass was left in the windows. Food was still very scarce, most of the Leningraders we met were pallid and emaciated from starvation and I wrote at the time:

The whole Leningrad region is a sight to make the angels weep. It is devastated like Flanders in the First War. For miles there is not a single tree. No bird sings. There is no place for a bird to rest. Nothing remains but leafless stumps, blasted off close to the earth by the artillery. All the historic palaces are in ruins. Peterhof will never rise again. Rastrelli's other baroque palace at Tsarskoe Selo is only a shell. Pavlovsk is devastated, Gatchina burned to the ground. The masterpieces of Rastrelli and Cameron lay right in Hitler's path when he lunged madly at Leningrad and, alas, they have been wiped off the face of the earth. Baranov, the city architect, speaks of restoring everything in time. But who will build afresh the agate chamber of Catherine the Great or the bedroom of the Empress Maria Alexandrovna with its violet glass and its floor inlaid with mother-of-pearl? Where in the world is another Rastrelli to be found?

Of course, I could not have been more mistaken. Baranov's prophecy is being fulfilled to the letter. Another Rastrelli has not emerged but ordinary Soviet craftsmen have contrived, with great expenditure of time and enormous sums of money, to acquire the skills of their eighteenth-century forebears with the result that Peterhof now looks almost exactly as it did before, Pavlovsk is restored and even the enormous Catherine Palace is being put together again. Next to the space programme, this labour of love must surely be the costliest operation now in progress anywhere in Russia. Leningrad now has a Metro second only to Moscow's in size and beauty and a rebuilding programme no less comprehensive, but this reconstruction of all the treasures of imperial Russia is something one cannot think that any other country would have attempted. If we in England had ended the war with Westminster Abbey, Windsor Castle and Hampton Court laid in ruins I believe public opinion would not have supported an attempt to recreate the past and post-war governments would doubtless have ruled it out as prohibitively expensive.

What is to be done with these magnificent palaces when they are fully restored is another matter. In the Catherine Palace at Tsarskoe Selo, which is very nearly 1,000 feet in length, they have partly solved the problem by opening a school of music in the section next to the church. When we arrived there on a crisp day of northern spring the strains of Mozart could be heard on the terrace, where gardeners were removing the stains of winter from the *parterres*, while the freshly gilded domes of the church dazzled the eye against a sky of almost the same rich blue as the palace itself. Rastrelli's architectural ornamentation is painted white in contrast but even the lavish Soviet treasury could not restore the original gilding of his caryatids and garlands. These are now rendered in a light brown colour. Many of the State apartments have been completely restored to their original condition; in others, one sees men at work in rooms stripped down to the original brickwork with gilded panelling and doors copied from the designer's drawings waiting to be put back into place. Several girl artists were to be seen lying flat on their backs on high trelliswork repainting the original designs of the ceilings. In the very English park, with its echoes of Capability Brown, most of the pavilions have been reconstructed but no attempt has yet been made to deal with the Chinese Village designed by Charles Cameron, the Scots Jacobite exile whose first commission this was for Catherine the Great. Families are living in some of the Chinese houses and their washing is flapping on the line but the rest of the village looks as ruined as it did in 1944. Bullet holes disfigure the walls, the Chinese dragons and birds on the roofs are twisted into grotesque shapes by rifle fire and the stucco has peeled away to the brickwork. Several more years of work lies ahead here. But Cameron's famous gallery is completely restored. At the point where this light elegant building joins the Rastrelli palace – that is where the whole scheme falters. Thus far one has accepted the baroque extravagance of Rastrelli as one accepts the Royal Pavilion at Brighton but from then on one begins to doubt one's own taste – and Catherine's. Cameron is so much better, so clear-sighted and austere, yet it is true that a whole palace in his style would not be a place fit for an eighteenth-century empress but rather for some ruler of a world state which hasn't yet been born.

Maybe Cameron's real strength was as a builder of trifles, a decorator, for when he built the palace for the mad Tsar Paul at Pavlovsk his hand was not so light – maybe because his patron's hand was heavy and already veined with madness, and the outcome must be considered disappointing from the outside though the interior is delightful. Most of the furnishings of Pavlovsk were evacuated before the Germans arrived so that restoration has not been so difficult as in the Catherine Palace and the suite of rooms occupied by Paul's widow, the Empress Maria Feodorovna, now looks as though their owner had only just stepped out of the french windows to take a walk in the park. On the upper floors at Pavlovsk is a fascinating exhibition of portraits and clothing belonging to the Romanov dynasty and their courtiers from the earliest times right down to 1917. Uniforms and dresses worn by the imperial family seem to gain in poignancy as they approach our own times. Gowns designed by Worth for the ladies of the families of Yusupov, Dashkov and Stroganov date from the *belle époque* down to the years of the first World War and family portraits range from Winterhalter down to John Singer Sargent.

After being exposed to so much splendour we drove back to Tsarskoe Selo – or Pushkin, as it is now called – in search of somewhere modest to eat. We passed the suburban station of Pavlovsk which is amusingly designed in a pastiche of Cameron's style – yellow walls and white columns with a golden spire borrowed from Zakharov's Admiralty by the Neva. In the main street of Pushkin a *stolovaya* was open. We had bortsch, black bread and cheese and a bottle of beer for 50 kopecks, or 4s. Around us park keepers and building workers seemed to have chosen a rather more elaborate menu for their midday meal but we fancied that our choice would have been their necessity in the days of the Great Catherine.

Moscow: home of Edmund Stevens

8 MOSCOW AGAIN

Moscow the second time round was like another city. May Day was approaching, and while we had been on our travels, the snow had gone, the trees had burst into bud and the city, no longer like one of those Anglo-Saxon peasants who used to be sewn into his underclothes for the winter, had cast a clout and put on summer raiment. One could well understand why *La Belle au Bois Dormant* is in Russia the best-loved of all the fairy tales: every year at this time comes the transformation scene which switches winter into summer without any tedious interregnum. Windows which have been closed for six months are thrown open and cleaned, flowers appear on sills repainted after a winter's grime has been removed. The frowsty old city fills its lungs with fresh air and no longer looks its age. At the National Hotel, Paul and I found we had gone up in the world and were treated with a new deference by the staff. We were given two of the best rooms overlooking the Kremlin. I was delighted to find myself in 305, which had an entrance lobby and a balcony, a sofa, dining table, two beds, a chandelier and some real old Tsarist rosewood furniture and a bathroom which contained a bidet bearing the imprint 'Trade mark, by order of Muir and Merrilees, Moscow', the old Scottish department store still in business under new management close to the Bolshoi Theatre. Many merry lees must indeed have passed this way since it was installed in 1908, at a time when the Island Race itself regarded the bidet with derision. A wall safe in which it had been intended that Madame should lock her jewels, *circa* 1902, had been painted over in the prevailing Wedgwood blue and on the wall there was a painting of a rustic huntsman gazing triumphantly down at the body of a fox lying bleeding in the snow. It was hard to believe that this had been painted only in the year before Stalin died: it could easily have been 150 years old. The food in the National was much better than it had been before. With the approach of May Day, the menu had been expanded. Pablo Neruda, the Chilean Marxist poet, was dining at the next table – the first of many V.I.P.'s winging in for the festival. We had an excellent dinner of caviare, and chicken à la Kiev, at a price well below the London level. Many ordinary Muscovites were anticipating the holiday by having an evening out among the foreigners. At our table sat a young couple who looked more like mistress and gallant than man and wife. A captivating little face, dead white with dark lashes and yellow eyes, it might have been painted by Foujita in the 'twenties. A feline character, too. When her husband was out of the room, Paul danced with her. She gave the returning husband a little grimace as though to say: 'Look at me – I'm well away!' The husband wore tired clothes and no tie but the wife was well dressed. The husband did not dance with her and she began to sulk. Having ascertained that they knew no English, we exchanged comments about them.

'Why is it,' asked Paul, 'that the most attractive women are so often bitches? Look at her – she's giving him the needle and the poor chap is suffering tortures.'

The husband told us in Russian that he was an engineer and that they had two children. I said that in London, my wife and I found it difficult to go out without anyone to look after our children.

'Ours are at home with the maid,' he explained with a touch of pride.

But their evening was not going well. The wife was eating a salad and drinking some brandy but the steak she had asked for was rapidly congealing and when I indicated this, she said with a pout: 'I don't really want it – he keeps ordering things I don't need.' It had cost, I noted, fourteen shillings. The husband, more and more unhappy, said it wasn't good to waste things.

'Get them to wrap it up then and take it home for the pussy cat,' she said.

'For the children at least. Don't let us be selfish.'

'I *feel* selfish,' said the wife. 'It's a holiday feeling.' She leant towards him and hissed something which I couldn't understand but which was evidently deeply wounding for the husband turned red, summoned the waitress and, in due course, had the remains of her dinner wrapped up in *Pravda,* ready to take home.

'Imagine doing that at the Dorchester,' said Paul.

'One has to admire her gall,' said I, 'and his moral courage.'

Paul brought out his sketch-book and began to draw her. He showed the first sketch to the husband while the wife was off dancing with an American. 'She won't like that,' the husband said. So Paul tried again while the wife twinkled at him. She pretended to be outraged by the drawing, saying 'You make me look like a soubrette at the circus' but you could see she was inwardly pleased for she folded up the drawing and tucked it away in her handbag. Paul had made her as pretty as he could without entirely deleting the mischief and malice without which her expressive face would have lost its character.

But their night out was not going well. The wife was now full of smiles and banter towards us but she paid little heed to the husband. He tried to relieve the tension by resorting to funny stories. The point of the first, which concerned the Second Coming, lay in the wide gesture with which the Jewish narrator ended the story – a second crucifixion being implied. His second story also had an anti-semitic trend and there could not be much doubt about their sentiments in general when Paul, sketching a man with an imposing black beaver at an adjoining table, inquired whether he was a foreign priest and was told by the wife: 'He's not one of us – probably a Jew.'

Not an admirable couple: the husband devoted but dour, the wife capricious, revelling in her power over him yet anxious to appear as a *femme fatale* who might have done much better for herself – it was Madame Bovary over again; as we left them to their brandy and their quarrelling, I wondered what her end would be. A neat ligature around that pretty little neck, perhaps . . .

★   ★   ★

The stage door of the Bolshoi is a sacred portal guarded by two bald-headed men of impressive masculinity though their functions resemble those of imperial eunuchs: no one gets in without a pass and no passes are issued except through the Ministry of Culture. Paul and I have passes that are in order but the ballerina who is taking us in has left hers in the pocket of her winter coat. She is a well-known member of the company but an unconscionable fuss is made before she is admitted. One wonders if she will have to go home and write out one hundred lines as a punishment. The reason for this strictness is entirely sound. Few dancers like to be watched at rehearsal while they sweat under the harsh lights in unattractive practice tights, nor does the management like the magic of the ballet to be diluted through the tittle-tattle of highly placed voyeurs. When Galina Ulanova was queen of the company she refused to rehearse before strangers in any circumstances, and the reigning prima ballerina, Maya Plisetskaya, will not have people admitted unless she is given their names in advance. We are well aware therefore that we have been greatly honoured and we walk down the scarlet-carpeted corridors past innumerable offices, dressing-rooms, rest-rooms and dining-rooms for the huge company with the diffidence of pilgrims who are about to be received by the Pope.

An opera rehearsal is in progress on the stage and we go up in the lift to the third floor where, in a huge room with the same raked floor as on the stage, the younger members of the company are exercising at the bar under the tuition of Elisaveta Gerdt, a famous old dancer now over seventy. The entire back wall where the footlights would be is covered in looking-glass so that the dancers may correct their errors. Four chandeliers hang from the ceiling but so rock-solid is the building that their crystals never sway, no matter how many dancers are cavorting beneath them. Presently, we go on to a similar room where 'the boys' class' is in session. Plisetskaya is the only woman among them. Her dark red hair hangs down in tight little pigtails. Plisetskaya hasn't quite sustained the promise of beauty that was evident when she was a dazzling strawberry blonde rather more than twenty years ago, but she does not look like a woman of forty. She is a very pretty little fox, trained to the pitch of an Olympic athlete. Asaf Messerer, whom I remember as a leading dancer, is in charge of her class: now bald and indistinguishable from a bus conductor as he sits in the director's chair, he suddenly becomes a dancer again when he jumps up, tightens the braces on his sagging trousers, and indicates with negligent grace the steps which he wants the class to run through. The male dancers are in the main small and wiry – not the tall athletic *danseurs nobles* one remembers from Ulanova's day – with the exception of one or two who look as though they might have come straight out of the Army. Plisetskaya is working with her usual partner, Fadecheyev, dressed all in black with a silk scarf round his neck, and when he steps aside to rest, she indicates by the lift of an eyebrow that one of the others should accompany her, and the young man who is selected moves to her side, a medieval squire called to duty by his queen. Presently a plump grey-haired lady in horn-rimmed glasses comes in to take a rehearsal of *Chopiniana* and Messerer cedes to her the chair of honour. I recognize Marina Semeonova who, even in 1943, was preparing to retire yet who still looked magnificent on stage at that time.

Natalya Besmertnaya moves in behind her. Plisetskaya prepares to leave the class, bows first to Messerer and then to Semeonova while Besmertnaya, before taking the stage, embraces the prima ballerina respectfully. Here one sees three generations of the ballet in transition. Plisetskaya knows full well that before many years have run, she will be in Semeonova's chair as a teacher while Besmertnaya will be reigning in her stead. The two active ballerinas, running with sweat as they work out, are obedient to the raised finger and, often, the raised voice of Semeonova – a grand but gay old lady now out of the race but compensated in good measure by the respect which is paid to her.

Besmertnaya is very thin and waiflike. Semeonova pulls her up mercilessly in mid-dance. 'Aïe, aïe, she's so young and she's becoming so old! Now, Natchinka, raise the instep . . . no, no, let's have it again . . .' a flow of Russian diminutives mixed with French technical expressions flows out of her. She drums the arms of her chair imperiously, swaying from side to side and chanting: '*Bolshoi klassicheski pas!*'

During a pause in the rehearsal, I am re-introduced to Semeonova who, with great charm, pretends that she remembers me which I am sure she does not, if only because I have aged far more disastrously than she has. What she has not forgotten is the book *Soviet Ballet* – 'All those wonderful things Iris Morley said about me! If ever one is depressed, one has only to take the book down from the shelf and return to those brave days again . . .'

'Now tell me,' she inquires, 'what do you think of my young lady?'

I say she looks like a child but has a wonderful clean line.

'She's not so young as she looks. By the time she's thirty, she should be right at the top.' Then, as Besmertnaya's partner carries her in a tremendous lift the full length of the stage, Semeonova cries out: 'See, she's another Fokine, only upside down.'

I am at a loss to understand this remark but sense in Semeonova's severe yet affectionate tone a desire to praise Besmertnaya and take her down a peg or two at the same time. One is impressed yet again by the arduous life of these dancers – the daily sweat-out at practice, the impossibility of ever letting-up or eating and drinking as one pleases – a lifetime of monastic dedication that pays a dividend of, at most, a few years of glory. Yet there is no trace of *Angst* or regret in the ebullient personality of Marina Semeonova. Why should there be? It must be rewarding, in one's late sixties, to be able still to play an honoured part in the greatest ballet company in the world.

★   ★   ★

From the Bolshoi, we went straight to another Moscow institution – the studio of the trio of satirical artists known as the Kukriniksy. On our way up Gorki Street, we passed the apartment of Ilya Ehrenbourg, whose walls are covered with the Impressionist paintings he collected during his many years in Paris. I used to visit him from time to time in the 'forties; we always spoke in French which induced him, no doubt, to avoid talking about contemporary Russia and reminisce about France instead. He told me many fascinating things about the French decline before 1939, of which he made use in his best novel, *The Fall of Paris*, but he was very ill-informed about England and indeed appeared, in a petulant sort of way, to dislike the whole Anglo-Saxon world, with the exception of its canine population. He was very fond of English dogs and in the worst days of the war shared his rations with a fox terrier. I had asked if we might pay our respects to him but he was not well enough to receive us and not long after I was told he had become very old and feeble and was not able to receive visitors. Shortly after this, he died.

The Kukriniksy live in one of the vast Stalin apartment blocks opposite the red and white pillared *Mossoviet* building. You pass under an arch and through a mean court at the back, then take a rickety lift, from which odd sections seem to have been removed for firewood, to the top floor. Here, the interior walls of a flat have been removed to give the artists a splendid studio. One of the trio was ill with heart trouble but the other two partners received us most warmly. One has a sharp Russian face rather like Gogol, the other a bluff seamanlike appearance. It is impossible to know just what contribution the three make to their joint *œuvre*. Paul believes that the sick one is purely an ideas man while the other two have grown so much together during the forty years in which they have been licensed jesters to the revolution that their styles have become identical. In the 'twenties and early 'thirties their satire was directed almost entirely against Soviet bureaucracy; after the rise of Hitler it was turned against fascism. This was the high point of their development and it is precisely here that their art seems to have come to rest, like the art of H. M. Bateman with 'The Guardsman who dropped it'. The Kukriniksy have always aspired to be serious painters. As Paul and I entered the studio, we admired what we thought was a Boudin but it turned out to be by one of the trio – they would not say which one. Hanging near it was a death mask of Mayakovsky, showing only three quarters of the face – large eyelids battened down, a strong jaw, the head of a very tall vigorous man. The rest of the face was not depicted for the most commanding of reasons – it had been shot away when the poet committed suicide. The best-lit wall of the studio was covered with an enormous painting which the trio had been

Leningrad: the Admiralty

working on for an exhibition to mark the fiftieth anniversary of the revolution. It depicts Goering, Hess, Keitel and the others in the dock at the Nüremberg trial when the films of atrocities which the German cameramen had themselves taken were being shown in the courtroom. Paul was put in a quandry when our hosts asked him what he thought of it. I could see him searching for adjectives which would not suggest a feigned enthusiasm and yet would not give offence. In this situation, artists are acutely sensitive to insincerity among their fellows. I thought the picture a cut above the Gerasimov realistic school and saved from being purely photographic because some of the Kukriniksys' sardonic raillery has spread itself, albeit thinly, across its many square feet of grey and brown paint.

The Kukriniksy brought out the drawings they had done on a recent visit to London and Paul produced some of his new Moscow drawings. We drank champagne and ate chocolates and oranges while this exchange was under way. Knowing that we were very hard up for roubles, these good-hearted fellows had also been active on our behalf among the editors of Moscow. *Literaturnaya Gazeta* telephoned to say they would like some of Paul's drawings. Within half an hour, one of their photographers came round. Paul's drawings were set up one by one on the Kukriniksys' easel and the photographer got them, in colour and in black-and-white, right away. Again the telephone rang. This time it was *Krokodil* wanting more of Paul's work – 'nothing pretty, of course, but any satirical sketches of Soviet types'. Their art editor soon appeared in the studio. We showed him drawings of Georgians in their aerodrome caps and old women in the GOUM department store. These went down very well and were bought right away.

How splendid, I thought, to be an artist and have one's work on show the moment it's completed. At that moment, all my work was still in my notebooks, or in my head.

*   *   *

Paul's most recent book, with Malcolm Muggeridge, was *London à la Mode* and from his researches for this book and also through the students he lectures to at the Royal College of Art, he has acquired a knowledge of 'swinging London' which made me feel an utter 'square'. My shaky knowledge of jazz had been gained at the Savoy Ballroom in Harlem before the war but Paul is something of an expert on the whole pop scene and we had often discussed how we should set about tracking down those manifestations of Pop which we had been assured existed, although well under cover, in Moscow and Leningrad. On our last night in Leningrad – a Saturday – the Astoria had been invaded by crowds of young Russians who outnumbered the foreign residents many times over. They had come to dance to the band which played there at the weekends. It was a good band, though traditional in manner, and the style of dancing it evoked was the somewhat restrained type one might see at Annabel's in London. The dancers were well-dressed young people – the men in dark blue suits, the girls in short skirts and very high heels – and they arrived in such numbers that the ballroom doors had to be closed after every table had been taken and piano stools had been brought in to give them seats at the bar where they could order drinks and supper. Many of them were drinking champagne. I said to Paul that the presence of so many bright young people in an expensive hotel filled with foreigners would seem to indicate that Leningrad does not possess anything like the kind of *discothèque* in which London is so rich. And indeed we had failed to find any. And yet as we strolled along the Fontanka and the Moika canals, we had heard familiar sounds of revelry coming out of private apartments there. New Orleans jazz, and the music of the Beatles and the Rolling Stones reverberated across the still canal waters. After all, anyone with a tape recorder can pick any music he likes out of the air and it was quite obvious that in the privacy of their own homes, this was the music which the young liked to dance to. But there seemed to be no public place where such music was played. And, of course, there are no buildings available for jazz clubs apart from the usual clubs for the young run by Party organizations.

Undeterred by this experience, however, Paul was determined to try again in Moscow. We questioned some students we met in the aeroplane and they told us that the place to go was definitely the Yunost Hotel. 'There,' they said, 'you will find the best jazz in Moscow and all the bright young people of the capital.'

The Yunost is an attractive modern hotel in the University quarter close to the Lenin Stadium. You approach it along the Komsomolsky Prospekt. We arrived there early but, because of the Russian habit of eating around the clock, the restaurant was already full and we took our places in a queue which formed at the entrance. The décor was Scandinavian, and a wrought-iron grille divided the restaurant from the entrance lobby. A rather surly *dvornik* who was on guard here told us we had little chance of getting in for an hour or so and he locked the gates so as to drive home the lesson. We forebore to flaunt our foreign status with a view to getting priority but two homely looking young women of the type one

Moscow Art Theatre

sees hanging around stage doors in the West approached us and asked if they might join us.

'Are you from abroad?' they inquired. 'Well then, tell the doorman and he'll have to find a place for you. But all the tables are for four people, you see, so we haven't much chance of getting in unless we can find two fellows to take us. Would you be so kind? Of course, we would pay our own way. We have plenty of money.'

I didn't relish the idea of being stuck with these girls for the rest of the evening so I temporised and we were saved in the nick of time by the *maître d'hôtel* who unlocked the grille and told us there were two places vacant at a table with two other men. We ungallantly seized this opportunity but we were soon wondering why we had bothered. The vodka was 'off', all dry wines were 'off' and so was a good deal of the menu. I thought the absence of vodka, in a place frequented by the young, might well be deliberate since it is supposed to inflame the passions but the one sweet Georgian wine available was almost undrinkable and the meat balls and chips we ordered were worse. Paul thought the band reminiscent of the Modern Jazz Quartet – a good sound and agreeable to dance to. The floor was soon crowded with dancers but they were not noticeably young or 'swinging', and we wondered if we had come to the right place. We asked our table partners – two young engineers from the Urals. They said the Yunost assuredly was *the* place for dancing: they had been recommended there themselves for a gay last night out in Moscow before they went home. We did not like to ask them if they were disappointed. But we certainly were. Why erect an iron grille to keep people out of so placid a playground? Architecturally, the Yunost was attractive but it deserved a better site. Goods trains clanking past the picture windows in the ballroom along the high embankment of the *ceinture* railway do not make for gaiety and the general atmosphere reminded us of nothing so much as Hendon on a wet Sunday night.

Fortunately, there is a Metro station right next door and we dropped into this, determined to get back to the city centre and order ourselves a decent meal before it got too late. At the Armenian Restaurant called Ararat, our luck changed. Shamelessly, we claimed priority in the queue waiting at the door as two foreigners who had just come back from the Caucasus and soon we were below street level in a smoky cellar where people were really enjoying themselves. The band consisted of six Armenians, by no means young: the singer was middle-aged and the pianist and flautist were white-haired but their music, in which tambourines took the place of drums, filled the restaurant with a dramatic resonance. We reflected that Russia is so rich in regional music that it is, perhaps, foolish to expect her to make a contribution to an art which owes its birth to the American Negro.

The Beatles and the Rolling Stones may well have added a new dimension to jazz which entitles English music to claim a share in the canon but, if so, this is a development which other cultures have not matched, nor is there any particular reason why they should.

★　　★　　★

All through our journey, Paul had been looking for 'good faces', by which the artist usually means old faces, since these are more interesting to draw than young ones. We had been told that some of the best faces in Russia were to be found at the House of Veterans of the Stage, a newly opened home for old actors on the Avenue of the Enthusiasts in a south-eastern suburb, and we were not disappointed. The home is maintained by the All-Union Society of Actors for 'lonely old artists who have no family'. It is named after the celebrated actress Yablochkina, who died recently at the age of ninety-eight and whose portrait occupies the place of honour in the entrance hall. The building stands in pine woods close to a hospital so that medical care is at hand when it is needed. It consists of a long block built in the shape of a crescent, entirely lined on one side with glass so as to provide a promenade where one can take mild exercise in bad weather. Living blocks open off this promenade at the rear containing 156 bed-sitting rooms with kitchenette and shower bath attached. The Veterans receive three meals a day in addition to what they choose to cook in their own rooms, clothes if they need them, and £6 a month for pocket money. Films are shown three times a week in their own theatre and actors from the Moscow theatres come to entertain from time to time, though one can scarcely imagine a more intimidating audience than this collection of old performers, many of whom were great stars in their time.

Paul and I strolled up and down the promenade in mid-morning, talking to people at random. The liveliest person we encountered was Lydia Nelidova, widow of the musician Feveisky, who was conductor to Chaliapine's opera company which flourished in the United States in the 'twenties. Mrs. Feveisky had been a dancer and later ballet mistress to Chaliapine. She last appeared as a dancer with Fokine in New York in 1940, after which she ran a school of ballet in

America. She took us to her room which was filled with her own flower paintings and studio portraits of herself in the 'thirties. While she sat on her divan to let Paul do her portrait, my eyes kept being drawn to photographs of a fashionable beauty in a cloche hat and strings of pearls, who evoked the days of the Charleston and of Cecil Beaton's early portraits of Paula Gellibrand and Tallulah Bankhead. Mrs. Feveisky had returned from America after her husband's death eleven years before. She had no children and no relatives living in Russia so she was glad to come to the House of Veterans. But then she appeared to be one of those vital women who project the spirit of *dolce vita* no matter where they find themselves. If Mrs. Feveisky's room resembled the dressing-room of a star player during a long run, that of her neighbour, Vladimir Gardenin, aged eighty-five, was monk-like in its austerity. Gardenin was trained by Stanislavsky at the Moscow Arts Theatre after graduating from Moscow University and he played Romeo and Hamlet at the Arts. But he gave up acting fairly early on to become a producer, travelling all over Russia to set up theatres in Georgia, Siberia and elsewhere. A signed photograph of Eleanora Duse held the place of honour above his bed. He also prizes a copy of the famous painting now in the Kremlin showing the leading actors in Russia posed together. Gardenin is one of these and Gennadi Uvarov, a very famous film star thirty years ago, is another. Uvarov, now seventy-nine and suffering from heart disease, occupies the room just across the passage. Mrs. Feveisky took us in to see him.

'He's suffering a lot of pain just now,' she said. 'He was asleep when you came but when I told him you were here, he insisted on getting up. Would you like to do his portrait? He's got a marvellous head.'

We found Uvarov sitting up in bed. A nurse had come in to give him an injection. As soon as she had finished, Paul began to draw him. The old gentleman was obviously delighted.

'A pity you find him like this,' said Lydia Feveisky, 'because usually we lead quite an active life. We play a lot of chess together. I paint pictures and he makes frames for them. Then sometimes I write poems – I'm a member of the Writers' Union – and he recites them beautifully – not just here, you know, but in a concert outside.'

Paul took a lot of trouble with Uvarov and Uvarov was pleased with the result. We promised to send the Veterans a copy of our book to place in their library. But, alas, after we had left them, Paul became dissatisfied with his portrait of Uvarov and tore it up. So Uvarov isn't in the book. And thinking back to the scene at his bedside and the painful way in which he drew breath, it seemed all too probable that by the time the book came out, he wouldn't be in the world either.

★   ★   ★

We had now been in Russia for nearly five weeks. Our time and money were running out and the moment of truth was at hand.

'Well,' said Paul, 'I've done enough work to fill a book and yet I've only scratched the surface. There's enough material in Moscow alone to keep me going for a couple of months more. But what about your side? Are you satisfied?'

'Far from it. I set out to take the temperature of Soviet life in as many different places as possible in the short time at our disposal, and we've done that and, of course, it isn't enough. And yet there is one thing that gives me great satisfaction and that is that one can now talk with Russians in a way that was never possible before. Twenty years ago, people were polite, they were even hospitable, but an invisible wall stood between them and us. There was no genuine contact, no real dialogue at all. Some of the old Potemkin spirit remains – we've experienced it, and not only in railway trains. But, taking the country as a whole, there isn't much of it left. And I think this opening-up and loosening of relationships between what was once a closed society and our own uncommitted world is the greatest, most beneficial thing that has happened in the years I've been away.'

I was able to strike this optimistic note because, with the tempo of our journey speeding up as it neared its end, I had lately found myself talking more freely to more people than I had ever done before.

An old friend named Anatol Shelepin came to see me. In Stalin's time, he may well have been licensed to have contacts with foreigners because he was regarded as 100 per cent reliable and no doubt his friendly surveillance of foreigners was useful to the Party. I had always regarded him as one of the best-informed men in Moscow and so he should have been for, although he was a journalist of minor gifts, he had been a sort of link man with the foreign community for over thirty years. The Americans, no doubt, would have set him down as a 'four-letter man' from the start but, since I never had any secrets to impart, I was not in the least concerned as to what use, if any, he made of my conversations with him. He could have 'bugged' the lot and lodged them in

Moscow: Re
Ararat Restaurant

the Lubyanka files for all I cared. On my side, he had always been worth listening to. And so he was today.

When I reminded him that I had left Russia at the end of 1947, he said: 'Then you missed the worst years. It was in 1949 that things began to go off the rails. At that time, I had it from one of the specialists in the Kremlin Hospital that the diagnosis made of Stalin's health when he had a check-up just before his seventieth birthday confirmed that he was suffering from mild paranoia. The "sickly suspiciousness" Khrushchev mentioned in his famous speech as having been always a part of Stalin's make-up had now become persecution mania. It was then that Beria – an evil genius if there ever was one, an absolute Iago, in fact – began to feed Stalin's mind with tales of non-existent conspiracies far more extreme than any he had produced before. And we now know that most, if not all, of the conspiracies Beria "discovered" even before the war were fabrications. Beria undoubtedly did this in order to make Stalin believe that he was essential to him and loyal above all others. In 1949, several members of the Jewish anti-Fascist Committee who had been key men during the war against Hitler were arrested and shot. One of these was Lozovsky, whom you probably remember as a deputy Foreign Minister.'

I certainly did. A natty little man with a red beard, he had always reminded me of Willie Clarkson, the theatrical costumier in London.

'And then,' continued Anatol, 'came the absurd doctor's plot, involving many of the best men in the Kremlin Hospital. Some were Jews who had been among the leading specialists in Russia in Tsarist times.'

'Is it true,' I asked, 'that there was any evidence of general anti-Semitism at that time?'

'No, you couldn't call it that. Despite all his defects, Stalin was always the most rational of men – he was never a racist and he had numbered Jews among his close colleagues and friends all his life.'

He then confirmed what I had been told by several Jewish friends of Russian origin whom I had consulted on this matter before I left London. These men I trusted because I had known them for many years and because they could have no possible interest in falsifying the picture. It is often stated that Jews are discriminated against by having to classify themselves as Jews on their internal passports and by having to submit to a quota for university entrance, such as used to exist at certain English public schools. Neither in London nor in Moscow could I find any evidence that the quota story is true. As to the passport – the history of this is complex. During

Lenin's time citizens were told at census-time that they could select whichever nationality they felt they had acquired. For example, a Georgian living in Leningrad could describe himself as a citizen of the RSFSR or a Jew in Kiev as a Ukrainian. But when Stalin became Commissar for Nationalities he insisted that nationality should be factually set forth. Otherwise, how would it be possible, in a multi-national state, to preserve the national integrity of Georgia or to prevent Great Russians or Ukrainians from settling in excessive numbers in, say, Uzbekistan and appropriating for themselves influence or office which should be reserved for the native inhabitants? This was logical enough in a union of republics wherein each nationality had its own 'homeland'. But the Jews, of course, had no 'homeland' save for the inhospitable territory of Birobijan where few Jews had any desire to settle. Thus many Jews ignored the regulations, especially those who had long since abandoned the practice of their religion. Ilya Ehrenbourg, for one, declared that though he felt himself entirely Russian in language and culture he would nevertheless put 'Jew' on his passport so long as Hitler continued his persecution of the Jewish people. Many completely 'assimilated' Jews followed his example. From about 1937, however, Beria insisted that all Jews, and indeed all other nationalities, should give a factual return. With the advantage of hindsight, both Anatol and my informants in London agreed that Beria might have been acting from anti-Semitic motives, though this was not apparent at the time. The result was that many thousands who might have escaped the Nazi extermination camps fell straight into them. On the other hand, a Jewish passport would often give a civilian priority in evacuation to a safe area as the Germans advanced. In the first census after Hitler's defeat the regulations were not changed: few bothered, for the horrific consequences of anti-Semitism seemed to have been obliterated for ever.

But has discrimination returned, now that Beria and Stalin are dead? Is it possible that the Soviet Government has forgotten the catastrophic results for Russia of calculated anti-Semitism under the Tsars which led to the emigration of millions of the most gifted and intelligent citizens? The American film industry is very largely the creation of Russian Jews: their contribution to the arts, to medicine and to commerce in America and Western Europe over the past ninety years has been immense. Is it possible that the present rulers of Russia have forgotten all this?

Henry Shapiro, who has been an American correspondent in Moscow for over thirty years, does not think so. A Russian Jew by birth, and now an American citizen, he believes that modern

Russians have outgrown the idiotic doctrine of anti-Semitism which was once deliberately instilled into them by Church and State. He told me that in his time he had never been conscious of anti-Semitism operating within Soviet society although, of course, individual anti-Semites exist in every country. In Stalin's last years, at the height of the Cold War, he had however been conscious of a strong official distrust of all citizens with foreign connections. And with an Israeli Embassy established in Moscow, no group of citizens was thought to have stronger foreign connections than the Jews. Zionism, he said, has always been distasteful to Communists because they calculated that it would lead to the subjugation of other peoples and to the setting up of a theocratic state. And they have come to regard Israel as an American-financed outpost of capitalism in the Middle East.

'You say there is no discrimination,' I said. 'But a Soviet Jew who at the height of the Cold War put the interests of Israel above those of the Soviet Union – would he not be discriminated against?'

'Certainly,' said Shapiro. 'He would have found himself in prison. Soviet citizens cannot have two countries, as pampered creatures like you and I seem to do. You can't be a Soviet patriot and a citizen of Israel at the same time.'

'Someone,' I said, 'ought to write an imaginary conversation on that point between Chaim Weizmann and Karl Marx.'

Aron Vergelis, the editor of the Yiddish monthly journal *Heimat*, is, naturally, a Communist who puts forward an orthodox viewpoint on Jewish affairs. Yet I found him worth listening to.

'These allegations about anti-Jewish developments in the USSR,' he said, 'are made for political reasons – not only by Jews but by politicians in search of Jewish votes.' Then he added with passion: 'As a Jew who went through the real war from start to finish, I tremble at the thought that people should still try to involve our long-suffering people in this disgusting Cold War. If it weren't for this propaganda, we Soviet Jews could have made more progress of late than we have. I don't deny we have problems here – but not *that* problem. The troubles we have arise from the great changes that have taken place within Soviet Jewry. A new physical image of the Jew has developed – his whole environment and way of life have changed. But the Jewish nation is still a very complex one, containing many points of view, and we are still searching for our individual way. Some of us want complete assimilation. Others don't.'

Before going to see Vergelis I had looked up some of those extraordinary writings couched in

Messianic terms which the Slavophiles produced in the nineteenth century. I wanted to ask him if they rang the same bell in his mind as they did in mine. We find Dostoevsky, for instance, writing in the journal *Time* just 100 years ago:

We believe the Russian nation is a phenomenon unique in the entire history of mankind. The Russian character is chiefly remarkable for its talent for universal reconciliation. The Russian sympathizes with humanity at large without distinction of nationality, blood or soil . . . he studies the spirit of foreign languages with all their finer points just as though they were his mother tongue. Who knows, dear foreigner, perhaps Russia was meant to wait until you have finished, so as to have time to grasp your ideas, to understand your ideals and aims and to give them a universal meaning and finally, free from all class or national interests, to move on to a new activity hitherto unknown to history, starting from where you have finished and carrying you all along with her . . .

And in a manifesto published at this time, he declared that the reforms of Peter the Great had damaged national unity by separating the Europeanized, educated class from the mass of the people who are the custodians of the national genius, even though the former never became entirely European at heart.

But now (and he was writing in the eighteen-sixties) *we all realize we cannot squeeze ourselves into the European pattern because we are different. We foresee that our future must be universal. The Russian idea, when it comes, will perhaps be the synthesis of all those ideas which Europe is developing with such stubbornness within its separate nationalities. Universal education in Russia will draw together 'the two nations' who were previously united only in the war of 1812 against Napoleon and when this unity dawns, Russia will set an example of enlightenment for the world to follow. The Russian zeitgeist will not be Christianity nor yet science, neither of which have united Europe; rather it will be a synthesis of all the Russian virtues which will act as a beacon to all mankind.*

I reminded Vergelis that these pronouncements – absurd though they seemed to liberal opinion at the time and to Marxists later – were part and parcel of the Slavophile movement which held that Holy Russia had a mission to bring true enlightenment to a materialist Europe and that Moscow and its Kremlin would one day succeed Rome as the centre of a regenerated world.

Vergelis smiled. 'So, you have a theory?'

'Simply this, that although Stalin was never an anti-Semite, the way in which the revolution developed during his thirty years of power must have created a very real, even if almost

sub-conscious, divergence between Russian Communists on the one side and Jewish Communists on the other. After all, the original contribution made by Jews to the Bolshevik Party was very great – Trotsky, Zinoviev, Bukharin, Litvinov, Lozovsky and many more. It is the essence of the great Jewish prophets – Marx, Jesus, even Freud – that their doctrine is universal. So when Stalin took the line that one could no longer wait for the world revolution Trotsky had counted on but must build socialism in one country without any foreign aid and at maximum speed before the capitalist powers could stage a second intervention, this amounted to a revision of Marxism on national, Russian lines, which must surely have been repugnant to many of the Jewish comrades.'

'To some of them, perhaps. But don't forget none of them were practising Jews and most of them saw in the long run that Stalin was right. *Socialism in one country* triumphed. Looking back, we can all see now that if we had waited for Bela Kun and Rosa Luxembourg and Thaelmann and Tito and Mao Tse-tung to help us on our way, we would never have got started at all.'

'My point is that the success of *socialism in one country* meant that those crazy maunderings of Dostoevsky and his friends were in the long run substantiated. Moscow *did* become the new Jerusalem – not of Slav Chauvinism but for Communists all over the world. The Kremlin came to exert a universal influence which only the Vatican had possessed before – and all this as a consequence of the Soviet Communist Party acting within the Russian national domain. Now surely it can never have been with such a goal in mind that Jewish intellectuals in Russia joined the Bolsheviks in such numbers? And when, with Nazi Germany defeated and Russia emerging triumphant with a whole string of like-minded governments as her allies, the state of Israel was set up mainly by Russian Jews supported by American power and money, one can well imagine the severity of the resulting trauma.'

'You are over-dramatizing matters,' said Vergelis. 'The Soviet Government favoured the setting-up of Israel. There are aggressive elements in Israel which have marred the image of the nation yet I think all Soviet Jews welcome the existence of Israel. Some of us have relations there and I think that if families want to be reunited, our Government ought to let this happen. But there are two and a half million Jews in the U.S.S.R. and I'm convinced that the overwhelming majority will never agree to leave this land. Ben Gurion made a fool of himself, you remember, when he said the six million Jews in America are only ten per centers and would only become one hundred per cent if they emigrated to Israel. But everyone knows this will not happen. Even the American Zionists, who support Israel up to the hilt, have no intention of actually living there. Why in Heaven's name then should these Cold War merchants suppose that we Soviet Jews are all panting to go to Israel? Would it be right in any case for us to go and seize the land of the poor Arabs when we have this vast and rich land to live in? Of course, they say, "You have only a few synagogues, you have no Jewish schools." What they mean is we have no *religious* schools. But such schools no longer exist for any of the peoples of the U.S.S.R. Our parents became atheists many years ago. I was a pioneer in Birobijan and went to a Yiddish school there and at Moscow University I was taught for two years in Yiddish, then in Russian. In Birobijan, there are now only from twenty to thirty thousand Jews; they still have a Jewish paper and theatre, even so. But in the rest of the country, the use of Yiddish is declining. And there's no incentive to go back to Birobijan because our people have put down roots where they are. There are a quarter of a million Jews in Moscow – about the same as in London. Now I'll tell you a strange fact of which I convinced myself after my journeys abroad; I believe there are actually two to three times as many Jews in the world as are officially registered as such. There's a tragic and curious thing – our community is eroding fast. Still, this doesn't apply to our best sons. In the new issue of *Heimat*, I have some drawings by Chagall. I correspond with him in France in Yiddish and he's never forgotten that he was born a Russian. In the same number, I've written a poem which says that wherever Chagall may wander, he lives under the sky of Vitebsk.'

My last engagement in Moscow before Paul and I caught the B.E.A. Comet back to London was one which could never in any circumstances have taken place before the Thaw set in. I was invited by a member of the Journalists' Club to meet him there for what he described as 'a drink and a really good talk, with no holds barred'. Knowing that I might want to reproduce some of our talk in a book, he asked me not to name him.

'Am I being unreasonable? It's not that I'm afraid to be quoted but I'm not a famous person, after all, and I'd only feel inhibited if I had to choose every word. And anything I might say would have only sociological interest, anyhow.'

I agreed to this proviso because, if the roles had been reversed, I would not have wished my bar-room talk to be reproduced in a Russian visitor's book, especially if I was going to be mis-quoted. The risk of mis-quotation here, however, was minimal. My host had spent a lot of time in America and his extremely fluent English was interlarded with New York slang.

'Call me after my mother's name – Grigoriev,' he said.

The Journalists' Club occupies yet another of Morozov's mansions – an Empire building on the inner boulevard painted buff with white columns and caryatids. The old building has been modernized within, with a bar, a beer cellar in the basement where – said Grigoriev – 'many a cub reporter has been down-graded for failing to hold his liquor as a journalist should' – a cinema, a room reserved for chess, a small theatre and a restaurant which appeared to serve food and drink all round the clock.

'How does this compare with the London Press Club?' he asked. I said it had rather the same Bohemian atmosphere but it appeared to be a wealthy club. How was it financed? By an annual subscription of 8 roubles from the 70,000 press workers all over the country. This provided an annual budget of half a million roubles – 'even so, you see, some bastards don't pay their subs' and he indicated a list of defaulters on a notice-board.

It was four in the afternoon when we entered the dining-room. I plaintively described the excessive hospitality of the Georgians but, alas, to no effect.

'You must try our Armenian brandy,' he declared. 'This is the stuff Winston Churchill went for – it's much better than the Georgian.' A bottle was placed on the table with some chilled Narzan water. I had hoped for a brandy and coffee but presently there came slices of lemon dipped in sugar, delicious baby cucumbers and then a steak with mushrooms – the speciality of the club. We did not rise from the table until three hours and a quarter later, having demolished the bottle of brandy.

My host was in his fifties, married twice, with one child, a boy of eleven.

'I can just remember the Tsar', he said, 'and how it all began. I had no education and never wore a tie – just an ordinary chap at the factory bench. My dad – he died three years ago – was an old Bolshevik but he used to be severe about Stalin – too rough, he always said. Yet he never went back on the Party. In the beginning, you know, we scorned money and good clothes as being bourgeois – all my generation did. We thought only about world revolution which we were sure was coming, though it never did. One Christmas, I got a big bonus and I bought myself a good suit and overcoat. After that, I began to be an intellectual. I went from the factory to college, got a history degree and went into journalism. Maybe I ought to have criticized Stalin too – but why should I? He never did me or my friends any harm – on the contrary, he opened up a new life for all of us. If he committed atrocious acts, I never saw them. So when Khrushchev made his revelations, I resented them. All very well to skin the bear when he's dead but Khrushchev loved the man when he was alive. Maybe we could have reached socialism by other methods, had

Lenin lived: he was a man of immense charm which he could have projected all over the country but he died and time was short and the road hard and we believed Stalin when he said a whole generation would have to sacrifice themselves so that the country could leap forward. And it *did* leap forward.'

Grigoriev plied me with many questions about my work and my family in England and then expressed concern lest I had not been given all the facilities I needed on my journey.

'Russia,' he said, 'has always been a difficult country for foreigners to penetrate and we still aren't as forthcoming as we might be. But, of course, we've had some nasty surprises when people who seemed perfectly friendly turned out to be outright spies – like that fellow Greville Wynne, for instance, outwardly a simple business man who was, in fact, the spy master of one of our worst traitors. Still, let me know if there's anything I can do for you and I'll try to do it.'

I pulled an inordinately straight face and said: 'You could put me in touch with the notorious British spy, Kim Philby.' And I told him about the old family friendship, adding that I had no desire to make a newspaper killing out of Philby or indeed to write him up at all but merely to talk with him as one would with any old acquaintance after a long separation. But, I added, perhaps he didn't know who Philby was?

'I've read about him – not in our papers, of course, but in yours, and I dare say I could get his phone number for you. I'll try anyhow.'

I am sure that Grigoriev did try, if only to substantiate his own image as a go-getting modern Soviet man. But Philby's familiar stutter never came through on my telephone. After the abduction of George Blake from an English prison, and given Philby's familiarity with the operas of Mozart, an uncommitted impresario such as myself might well have appeared to him as the potential director of an *Entführung aus dem Serail* in reverse.

Grigoriev said he supposed spies were a necessary evil but the only one for whom he had respect was Sorge, the Soviet spy inside the German Embassy in Tokyo. 'There,' he said, 'is a man we can all be grateful for. He was able to tell us positively that the Japanese would *not* attack us if the Germans crossed the Volga and so we were able to bring back the divisions from Siberia who, arriving in the nick of time, delivered the knock-out blow at Stalingrad that saved us all.'

We spoke about books in general. He had never heard of Evelyn Waugh. I said: 'Get someone to translate *The Loved One* into Russian. It's one of the finest pieces of satire since Swift.' A methodical man, he made a note of this. He had never heard of Aldous Huxley or George Orwell

either but he had read all the James Bond books in English and had strong views about them.

'To my mind,' he said, 'they're quite harmless. It's silly to call them fascist or reactionary – they are only meant to entertain.'

But he was fascinated to learn that Ian Fleming had been a friend of my youth, and pressed me to tell him what Fleming had been like. 'A solitary,' I said, 'but an affectionate friend.' By an odd coincidence, a well-dressed man at a nearby table looked very like Ian, though his hair was white, as Ian's would be now if he were still alive. I, in turn, wanted to know who this sibling was. No one important, I was told – just one of our members who comes from Leningrad.

'Tell me what *you* have written', he said, 'and I'll get it out of the Lenin Library.'

I returned the compliment, and he said: 'I'm still hoping to write the big book all journalists long for but I don't suppose I ever shall. I want to do America in depth, the way de Tocqueville did, only from the viewpoint of a modern Soviet man. It would, as you say, "take the mickey" but not too much because I like a great deal of America and I can't feel hostile even to their institutions though they produce such sorry results. But, unfortunately, I've just turned down a second job in America because it would mean leaving my son in boarding school here and I don't like such places. Who can say what associations he might form so young? I don't want him to be neglected, as some of our kids are, you know, and grow into a delinquent. After living in America, I think I can understand the cult of L.S.D. and instant sex and way-out clothes. Some of the best of the young in all countries are in revolt against their respective establishments. Yours wear long hair and peculiar clothes – and why not? This seems to me a form of idealism. The young want no part in a society that seems to them to be drifting towards annihilation. But, of course, these revolts don't endure because the women don't support them. A girl today may give herself to a man she hardly knows but that's not how she really wants to live – women want real love, they need continuity and true affection. They can't raise children in a society from which such things are excluded.'

I asked him to what extent the spirit of revolt was present in Russia. He said: 'Mayakovsky, you know, used to wear a woman's yellow pullover and when they asked him why, he would say: "So as not to look like you." But he despaired too soon and committed suicide. Today our young poets also feel the winds of revolt but they are not beatniks or hippies – they like to wear good clothes. We are a more mature society than we were in Mayakovsky's day and if our desire for change is expressed in a more reasoned way, this is because we now have a large intellectual layer in society – more numerous, perhaps, than in any other country. We know that drugs and sexual anarchy solve nothing. That's why I personally have a great admiration for your Beatles: they sing of real love, of the beauty of constancy – precisely what women most desire and so all the girls adore them. Our press was very foolish at one stage to attack the Beatles – I am quite sure they are on the side of the good and the true.'

Grigoriev spoke a great deal about England.

'Yours is an extremely adult country, the first ever to dissolve a great empire in a friendly and sensible way. I have been in India and I know how the Indians admire their former oppressors. You have been very clever. You have left all these countries in good time and, in many of them, you are genuinely missed. You will derive great benefits from this as time goes on. The contrast between British reason and American unreason in getting into a big war in Asia where nobody wants them is not lost on the world.'

'Are these your personal views or do you think many Russians feel the same?'

'I believe most intelligent Russians feel as I do.'

'In that case,' I said, 'it seems a pity that such sentiments are never expressed in *Pravda*.'

'Well,' he said, 'we have an ideological posture which we have to maintain just as your leaders are constantly affirming their loyalty to the American alliance when one knows quite well that intelligent Englishmen would very much rather be independent, as they used to be. But there is a great deal of goodwill here towards the English. There is simply nothing for us to quarrel about; it's hard for us to imagine any circumstances in which England and the Soviet Union could fight one another – so long, that is, as England remains what she has always been. But if England were ever to fall under the complete domination of America and became just one of their United States, then from our viewpoint, that would be a point of no return, a moment of danger. It would extend the American frontier three thousand miles to the North Sea and the Orkneys. But I don't think that's likely to happen because, in America too, there is a liberal intelligentsia which is growing in numbers. I mean the people who defeated McCarthy and then supported Kennedy. Let us hope there are enough good liberal minds in our three countries to keep our governments on the right lines.'

I asked Grigoriev what he thought of the present Soviet leadership.

'I think they are doing reasonably well. Mind you, there's not a single great statesman among them but no country can produce men of the highest calibre to order. I don't think we will ever

give another man as much power as Stalin possessed but if – despite all his power – Stalin was at heart a cautious man and I think his record shows that he was, then I don't think we need fear any incautious acts from the present leaders. But if ever they were to lose patience and take risks, then the Party would have to try another combination, as we did after Khrushchev was dropped and as we might have done before Stalin's intelligence became clouded. Did you know Stalin had offered to resign at one point after the war? But everyone was so bedazzled by him that the idea seemed unthinkable. Whatever happens, though, methods of compulsion are no longer needed in this country. Stalin was racing against time and he only just made it before the Fascists attacked. But no one dare attack us now; we are a different country and the world knows it. Mao is a foolish old man who is trying to divert the course of history but the Chinese are a highly gifted people and they will prevail.'

'You are, then, an optimist?'

'About people, yes. Our own people are at bottom religious, you know. I don't mean they are Christian but they have a strong sense of morality, of what makes for good. Their instincts are not aggressive. You will never find the Russian people fighting for worthless causes in distant lands, nor even for good causes, I might add, and we haven't the slightest desire to become World Policemen. After all, ours is a splendid country filled with wealth of every kind and we have the chance to build here the most advanced civilization that has ever been seen. With us, it is going to be *Communism in one country* – bothering about bits of Africa or the Americas would just be a senseless diversion. Sometimes, of course, one gets moments of depression when one imagines some lunatic in Germany, or maybe China, committing the world to total destruction but believing in Man as we do, we Communists must believe that Reason will triumph. If the bomb falls, of course, we have this little anecdote . . . After ages of time have elapsed, a man in a cave one day picks up a couple of sticks and starts to rub them together. His woman snatches them out of his hand and says: "For God's sake, don't start it all over again . . ." '

160

—